The Names of My Mothers

Dianne Sanders Riordan

"Nancy, George, and Miss Betsy Sanders" by Margaret Maron as it
appears in "The Clue in the Diary"/by Carolyn Keene; illustrated by
Russell H. Tandy; with an introduction by Margaret Maron.
- Facsimile ed. 1994. Reprinted by Applewood Books.

Cover Photograph: the original family farmhouse, 1889.
It has been included in the National Historic Register since 2001
and dates back to 1852.

Produced by:

FriesenPress
Suite 300 – 852 Fort Street
Victoria, BC, Canada V8W 1H8

www.friesenpress.com

Distributed to the trade by The Ingram Book Company

Table of Contents

We shall not cease from exploration
And the end of all our exploring
Will be to arrive where we started
And know the place for the first time.

T.S. Eliot
"Four Quartets"

This is not a story of regret.

Nor is it in any way a repudiation of my adopted life.

But knowing is a holy thing

And it is in *knowing* that one comes home.

Dedicated

to *all* my mothers

Anonymous

She was born when no one was lookin'
While paint peeled from the ancient farmhouse
And wooden swings swayed idly
Beneath gnarled crepe myrtles.

She was born
While tobacco dried in the sun
And bolls of cotton stood dampened by dew
Ready for harvest.

She was born while uncles and aunts
Fished placidly in the pond beyond the barn
Weavin' stories from clouds
Plannin' picnics, parades and endless church suppers.

She was born in the cool of a Northern sky
On the cusp of autumn
While steamy heat radiated
From her granny's tin roof.

She was born while her mother wrestled in vain
Tethered on a table beneath cruelest lights
Her labor long
Bloody with hemorrhage.

She was born -
But no one was lookin'

Dianne Sanders Riordan
[Inspired by the poem "When She Got Born" by Marjorie Norris]

Prologue

"Mom. Please. Pull over," my daughter says, her voice insistent. "You've traveled a lifetime to be here. You don't need to be distracted by driving."

Without a word, I pull to the side of the road. Aimee and I change places and continue eastward on Highway 70, the surroundings flat and nondescript. *A lifetime to be here...*

We have just entered Johnston County, North Carolina. An unimposing sign tells us so. Johnston County. A place I never knew existed until about a year and a half ago. Johnston County—with its towns of Selma and Clayton, Benson and Four Oaks. We drive through each of them, taking in their smallness, their quiet country atmosphere. A sign announces Smithfield, population seven thousand five hundred and ten, and I feel my entire body jump to a new level of awareness. Here dwells my family. My blood family. Aunts, uncles and cousins of all degrees live here. But of crucial significance, my *mother* lives here—one among the population of Smithfield's seven thousand five hundred and ten. My mother, a person whose identity was unknown to me until so very recently.

A lifetime to be here. And with this thought framing all my actions, Aimee and I continue following the signs that lead us to the heart of this small town.

Chapter One

How can I pinpoint the beginning of this journey? Haven't I always dwelt in the land of journeying? Wondering always. Discreetly, silently searching every face I see, calculating height and weight. Vigilant always. Considering the possibility that someone might resemble me—be *kin* to me. The wondering as much a part of my being as my dark brown eyes and hair.

Where did they come from, these features of mine? Features so very different from the ones who called me daughter. These features that brand me as different from all I call family.

Helen, my adopted mom. Whose pale blue eyes looked out from a face more round than not. Whose lightly freckled, slightly turned-up nose belied her years and gave her a look of perpetual innocence, open and pleasant. Her sandy hair was straight and fine. "The bane of my existence," she'd ruefully complain. Helen, her hands her talent. Tiny hands, ring size four, blue veins pulsing as she would competently roll out her hallmark pie crust or refinish a needy chair.

Bill, my adopted dad, seemed oversized somehow. Even in his elder years when weight was lost, his manner still projected a kind of *bigness*. His hands, huge and capable. Calm blue eyes smiled in a face broad and sturdy that bespoke his French and German heritage. His thin brown hair balding ever since I can remember.

I was never calm, like Bill. Never sweet, like Helen.

I turn my eyes to Aimee's hands, resting easily on the steering wheel, seeing in her dear face both the present and the past. It is good that she is with me, this child who most resembles me and is most like me in temperament and talent.

—

1

It had always pleased me to think of Aimee's birth. The where and how of it, the wonder and joy of it. Each detail deeply etched in memory. Even the names of the doctors and the nurses. A legacy of memory. Precious. Shared over and over. Aimee's legacy. *Her* beginnings.

I had missed that growing up. My birthing story. Somehow it wasn't enough to know that my parents drove to an orphanage and picked me up. I wanted to know more than that. Especially how I got to that place in Lackawanna, New York. And I guess, more than anything, the *why* of it all; why I was given away.

And so, restless with a need to know, deep and relentless, I searched. I searched for answers and for a mother who, though lost to me, was yet profoundly present. I searched because I could no longer *not* search. And when my every effort led to doors both closed and locked, I found a woman who said that she could do what I had not been able to do. Her name: Christine Lee. Her profession: Kinsolving Investigator.

"I have found your mother," her voice, over the telephone, was gentle. "I have found her, and she is alive."

It was my birthday. My fifty-second birthday.

Overwhelmed by the power of those simple words, spoken on the twentieth of September, 1995, I sat at my dining room table, transfixed. Writing over and over the name I had just been given.

Elizabeth Sanders
Elizabeth Bynum Sanders

My mother's name. And beneath it, I wrote my own. That name given to me at birth by my mother-just-found. *Susanne Sanders,* I wrote ...*daughter of Elizabeth Sanders.*

And I wept.

Chapter Two

I called her that night. The night I was given her name. Found out she was alive. Perhaps, if it had not been my birthday, I would have done things differently. I might have written her a letter first, to somehow prepare her. Maybe I would have used an intermediary, found someone to be a go-between. To lessen the impact. To soften the shock she would surely feel.

But it didn't happen on a different day. And so it felt as if I were in a play, the script of which had already been written.

"Mom," my son Fran had said. "Mom, your heritage! You'll receive your *heritage* on your birthday!"

And so more by instinct than thought, I called—it was the hardest call I have ever made.

It was not yet dark when I finally picked up the phone. Somewhere in the background I could hear dogs barking and children calling to one another in play. Strains from a Beethoven symphony filtered from a neighboring home. I sat cross-legged on the pale green rug centered on the hardwood floor of our den. Drawing courage from all that was familiar, I dialed, touching each number deliberately. In two rings she answered. I wasn't ready for her to answer.

"Hello."

It was a woman's voice—a quiet voice, soft and lilting. A voice that accented the first syllable of her greeting.

"Is this Elizabeth Sanders?" I asked, my words spoken as if this were a casual call.

"Yes, it is."

"My name is Dianne Riordan," I said, pressing on. "I'm calling from Clarence, New York. Is this a good time for you to talk?"

"Yes, this is a good time."

And suddenly I found myself unable to speak.

The pounding of my blood filling my ears, I somehow stuttered the next words:

"I was born on this day at Our Lady of Victory Hospital in 1942," I said. "My mother named me Susanne."

Silence followed. An unbearable silence. *Oh God, please don't let her hang up*, I prayed, my hands clenched tightly against my chest.

"What do you want from me?" Her voice was now harsh and defensive.

The rush of my words poured out from a thirst I only barely understood.

"Oh, I don't want anything from you," I breathed. "I only want to know that you're okay. I want you to know that I'm okay and that I have always loved you."

A profound stillness overtook both of us. I could feel its presence pressing like a shroud as I waited for her to answer.

"I have always prayed for you," she said, her voice carefully breaking the glassy surface of the moment, trembling with the unexpectedness of this improbable, impossible call. And with her answering voice touching the depth of me, I felt myself transported, merging with all that was good and pure and right in the world. I started laughing, because there was nothing else I could do. And then I heard an answering laugh. It was the first time I ever heard my mother laugh. It was more like a chuckle, amused and light. And I felt both relieved and comforted.

"Well," she murmured. "This is a call I have dreaded. All these years…" And her voice trailed off.

Then, with a tone more practical and down to earth, she invited my questions, and I became more deeply aware of her Southern way of speaking, so soft, melodious almost, with an ageless quality of gentility and good manners.

My roots are Southern. How strange, I thought.

"What do you want to know?" she asked with an almost gentle familiarity, and I could sense her forthrightness.

My words tumbled one after the other, words tripping over a heart that wanted to say, *I love you, Mother* and longed for a response in kind: *I love you too, and oh, do you want to get on the next plane and come see me?*

Instead, I asked, "My nationality. What *am* I?"

All my life I had struggled with this question. Hadn't I always imagined myself to be of Italian descent, or maybe Greek or Spanish? At one point I was sure I was a gypsy and filled the blanks of this great mystery with a never-ending, but still somehow unsatisfactory, adventure.

Recently, I'd been content to call myself Mediterranean. That suited me, and I was *almost* satisfied.

Her answer, however, was more satisfying than the most romantic of fairy tales.

"On your Grandmother Peterson's side, you are Irish, with a bit of Scotch. And on your grandfather's side, you are English."

Irish! English! Scotch! *Your grandmother. Your grandfather.* And I wanted her to repeat those words. Words that were taking me in. Connecting me to a whole heritage, to a people who lived and breathed and were my people by *blood.* My whole body tingled, as if the blood circulating through me was being recreated. I felt as if I were being born in a whole new way, and I found myself touching my features to see if they were still familiar. I felt myself becoming real, enfleshed, as she continued to tell me about my family, about aunts and uncles and cousins, about Smithfield and the family farm.

I listened carefully, straining to catch each phrase. Every nuance and shading important, loving the very sound of her. I listened as her tone became more somber. Darkening with regrets and buried memories.

"You'll want to know about your father," she said. "His name is Kenneth Whitney, and he was stationed at Fort Bragg, the Ninth Division. I was a waitress at the Service Club on the base, and we hit it off right away. Pearl Harbor happened..." She hesitated, then continued with a deep sigh.

"We were to be married before he had to ship out. But I found out he had been married before, and he hadn't told me, and so I could never marry him.

"A priest friend, Father Higgins, knew about Our Lady of Victory Home just outside of Buffalo, New York. And so I told Mother and Daddy that I had broken my engagement and was going to go north to work for the war effort.

"I stayed in Buffalo for almost three years after you were born." She paused only a moment. "I never did marry. Never cared to after that."

And there it was. My *beginnings,* at least the bare outlines of them. A gift unwrapped word by pain-filled word. The very speaking of her truth causing both of us to become more visible. Light replacing shadows and years of pretending.

"I named you Susanne," she said. "After Susan Anne, my favorite sister. Susan is my 9-1-1, my confidante and my best friend. She lives across the street from me. I don't know what I would do without her."

"I like the name, Susanne," I said.

But inside I trembled. A namesake. I was my Aunt Susan's namesake. Named *for* someone. Not just a word snatched from a melody of a once popular song: *I'm in heaven when I see you smile. Smile for me, my Diane.*

Oh yes, I was smiling then, smiling with the knowledge of my first name.

Night fell softly, imperceptibly as we spoke. Only her voice mattered. Her words. Just the two of us this precious night. The palest of moonlight brought deepening shadows, heightening my growing sense of shelter, of protection. The room became my mother's womb, and I never wanted to be without her again.

"Are you married?" she asked. "Do you have children?"

The question startled me, and I sensed she would be disappointed if I did *not* have a family, was *not* married.

"I have been married for almost thirty years," I said. "My husband's name is Frank. We have seven children, three daughters and four sons."

"*I* have *seven grandchildren!*"

"And two great-grandchildren," I whispered.

I could feel her heart expanding as she struggled to absorb my words. How overwhelmed she was. How overwhelmed was I.

Chapter Three

Love is stronger than fear or time
And cannot be terminated
Or legislated
Or denied.

j. fruland

I was euphoric those first days after contacting Elizabeth. Irrationally, outlandishly euphoric. And I sang the song of Elizabeth to all I met. Stranger, friend—it made no difference.

I so appreciated Frank's kindness to me that memorable evening. He took our youngest son, Matthew, to our son Chris's volleyball game so I could make my improbable phone call in total privacy. And then, later, went with me to a local pub, listening attentively as I began to unwrap the mystery of what I had discovered. He listened as I sketched for him his newly found in-laws—my own blood family of aunts and uncles and numerous cousins. And for him, the dimension of a *second* mother-in-law after twenty-nine years.

He let me ramble about the family farm and Fort Bragg and why my mother didn't marry my father. Retelling a story told simply, by a woman whose telephone voice changed from curious to defensive to warm to pain-filled to matter-of-fact. Who answered question after question and asked me some of her own. I only knew that I loved the voice and I loved the woman and I loved my husband for letting me speak about her and not getting impatient when I repeated myself in the telling. My tongue tripping and skipping and stuttering as I scrambled to remember each minute detail, embedding them in my being through the speaking. Then, he listened to my silence.

I awoke the next morning feeling both graced and graceful. I felt like a cock-eyed optimist and Mary Poppins rolled into one. I moved with ease, light-hearted and light-footed, and called each of my away children – Danielle in Arizona just beginning her law career, and the boys at their colleges - and as many friends as I could reach. I even told the shop-keeper at the gift boutique where I agonize over the right card to send to her. It was impossible to be quiet. I wanted the whole world to know that I had been lost and now was found. I was like a teenager caught in the throes of first love and wanting everything to be perfect.

I spent the whole day rummaging through albums, looking for photographs of each of us separately and all of us together, photos that would be so attractive and so irresistible that she would want to jump aboard a plane and come meet us.

Dear Elizabeth, I wrote, because I didn't know what else to call her. She went by Miss Betsy, Christine Lee had told me. But to address her as Betsy didn't feel right. Nor could I say *Dear Mother*. Not yet. And so I called her Elizabeth.

My words flowed without effort, and I carefully copied them onto ivory rice paper, signing my name with deliberate, painstaking strokes. I felt like a schoolgirl trying to make a good first impression on a favorite teacher. I placed the chosen photographs inside the card, its cover splashes of blues and greens framing softly mounded sand dunes and sea grasses. I sealed the envelope with a kiss, fervently praying that she would answer me soon.

I mailed the letter September 22nd. I did not hear from her for an entire month.

Chapter Four

Her answer arrived without fanfare or fireworks of any kind—one envelope among many placed unceremoniously in our mailbox by a mail-lady unaware that she bore tidings of great import. My breathing quickened as I separated my mother's letter from all the other pieces of mail, clutching it protectively. I stared at the envelope for a long time before opening it, absorbing every detail.

The return address pictured a white sailboat, skimming on a shiny blue background. The stamp showed a conch shell and two tropical fish, one large, one small. Her writing was sharp and no-nonsense, reminding me of my Great-Aunt Bertha's penmanship. I liked the crisp way she formed her numbers, and knew I would keep this letter and its envelope forever. A treasury of clues, helping me form an image of this mother-woman I'd yet to meet. I hoped there would be pictures inside.

I retreated once more to the den, where I made my first phone call to Smithfield, pillowing myself among the cushions of the sofa to read my mother's first words to me.

Dear Dianne,

Please don't give up on me. I am not intentionally ignoring you. My mind is in such turmoil that I can't put my thoughts in perspective to express my emotions. I am bewildered that my innermost secret has been revealed. I have never confided in anyone.

Your letter was consoling in the knowledge that you had a good home life, a good marriage and a very wonderful family. I have a lump in my throat when I look at the pictures. I am not insensitive to the fact that they are my grandchildren. The names of all of you are in my heart.

Tears come easily to my eyes when I look at the pictures and think of you – I do see myself in your graduation picture.

I am eternally grateful to the couple who took you as their own to love, cherish and nurture you to be the outstanding daughter, wife and mother your letter reveals you to be. How nice you weren't an only child.

This isn't my first attempt to write you. It must be because I am such a coward. This is something I never dreamed of being confronted with, and I am having a problem facing it.

You must realize there was no joy in my pregnancy. I had severed my relationship with the man who shared your conception and separated myself from family and home. I accepted the advice of my spiritual adviser and the nuns I came in contact with at OLV. Everyone was kind and I had no bad experiences except maybe homesickness at times, especially when I would receive a letter from mother.

My rule has always been yesterday is past, live today and tomorrow will take care of itself. Not so – yesterday can catch up with you and change the future and what has been done cannot be erased. Believe me, nothing you have said will hold me back now that our relationship has been discovered to each other.

I do thank you for your letter, the pictures and the "run-down" of your beautiful children. What a wonderful family! My only part is that I gave birth to you. I am so remorseful that you were born out of wedlock. My prayer for you has always been for you to have a good life.

Please be patient with me. You threw me a fast ball, and I haven't recovered from the shock. I do love you and pray for all of you.

Elizabeth

Her words slowly sank in, filling spaces once barren. I drew my knees to my chest, gathering myself in an embrace, wanting to call and hear her voice. Wanting, even more, to feel *her* arms around me. I needed to be gentle with myself and nestle further into the quiet. I hoped she would be gentle with herself as well.

Samson nudged open the door to the den and, with exaggerated nonchalance, nipped my toes. She purred loudly, anticipating a treat. Ordinary times once more.

Chapter Five

Pictures came the following day. I could feel their edges through the thinness of the envelope I held in my hands. Without ceremony or hesitation, I slid into my chair by the kitchen window where sunlight streams, softening my surroundings. With care, I opened the letter, my thoughts racing. *She has sent me herself. Her own image and likeness. My image, too? My likeness? My children's? Will I like what I see? Will she seem familiar to me?*

There was a short note wrapped around the photographs.

I hope you will like these pictures. Love, Elizabeth.

I took the first photo in my hands. It was in black and white, dated 1951.

> *This is me with Robert Barbour, my sister Susan and her husband Glen's oldest, and Mary who is my brother Bill and his wife, Virginia's oldest. The boy in the background is the adopted son of my sister Mary. He was born in April of 1942—the same year you were born. He left her when he was 17 and was never heard from since.*

My mother was thirty-eight in the black and white photograph and looked about twenty-five! Her hair was short and wavy, brushed casually behind her ears. A runaway curl danced above one eyebrow. Her smile was easy, and my cousins rested snugly on her lap. A sense of jealousy mixed with curiosity rose within me as I gazed on my cousins' ease with Betsy. I wondered about the unnamed adopted cousin and why he ran away, and for a moment I fantasized that Aunt Mary had adopted me instead and knew I would not have run away.

I was startled as well because Elizabeth reminded me not of myself, but of my daughter, Erika, and my son, Tim. Her face was narrow, and her eyes were set closer together than mine. My mother's face a mirror for my children. A touchstone. A connection weaving itself not only in and through *my* life, but the life of all my children and grandchildren—and all who would come after them. No longer did their heritage contain a void. No longer were there simply questions. Tim resembled my mother, and Erika did as well. And knowing this made a difference.

—

A boa constrictor rested on my mother's shoulders in the next photo, dated December, 1951. It was taken in Daytona Beach, Florida, and I thought of a similar picture of Erika with a snake fearlessly draped across her twelve-year-old shoulders at a picnic on a beach in Guantanamo Bay, Cuba, where we were once stationed. I smiled at the memory and couldn't wait to share the picture with all my children. Their grandmother wearing a snake—it would delight them as much as it had delighted me.

—

"Lillybet - Farmer's Day, 1952" captions the next image.

The lady who wrote the caption is the only person to call me Lillybet. I led the parade carrying the flag in the last Farmer's Day parade.

She looked jaunty in this photograph. Completely at home on horse-back. Her crisp white blouse and dark riding skirt a striking contrast to the light mane of the horse she rode. I wondered if the horse belonged to her, or at least to the family, and thought of how my girls had always loved horseback riding. I wondered how my mother was chosen to lead the parade and what exactly was Farmer's Day, anyway? So much to know. So much to learn. For the moment I was happy, simply loving her spirited expression—her face so open and relaxed.

—

Mother and me taken when visiting my sister Mary in Tampa, Florida. 1954. Mother died December 31, 1966.

Here was a picture of my grandmother. Betsy stood next to her, her arm resting easily on her mother's shoulder. She appeared to be stern, my grandmother. I wondered what she was like and what my cousins called her, and if she was good to them.

—

"Lillybet's 50th birthday party. November 25, 1963."

At the home of Willy Wright, my friend and work companion. She put me in a rocking chair with a cane, a shawl, a sunbonnet, a corncob pipe and an apron. She said no more shorts or going bare-legged and bare-footed again.

I doubt that Betsy listened.

—

"August 25, 1968."

An absolutely radiant Elizabeth stood by the door of her blue rambler station wagon. I thought it curious that a single woman would choose to drive such a big car and couldn't wait to ask her why.

—

"Christmas, 1971."

Betsy sat on a brown leather couch, an afghan of crocheted stars neatly positioned on the back cushions. Her hair appeared blonde, but her words written on the back of the photo tell me: "I wasn't a blonde - my hair is getting white." I wondered if my hair would be white by my late fifties. Knowing that her hair was white at that age made the reality of early gray or even white all right by me. *After all, it's in my genes*, I thought and smiled with the knowledge. "It's in my genes!" I shouted out loud to Samson who had settled on my lap.

—

"5/18/88."

A picture taken at Olin Mills of my mother with her sisters, Martha and Susan, and her brother, Bill. A simple notation of their dates of birth, and in Martha's case, the date of her death. She had died just over a year ago, and I felt sad that I would never meet her. My aunts and uncle were gathered around my mother in this more formal picture. Elizabeth, second oldest of six. Only Susan and Bill still alive. Would Betsy tell them about me?

—

"Taken in front of St. Ann's Church in Smithfield, NC - April 9, 1989."

Here my mother stood with a red hibiscus in her hand. Her hair was now completely white, still short and wavy. She wore a white wool blazer. A blouse of deepest turquoise seemed to match the blue of her eyes. A silver brooch intrigued me. It was intricate, unusual. It looked like a pin I might have chosen.

—

She looked fragile in this most recent photo and it was more than six years old—I felt an urgency growing within me to meet her face-to-face.

Chapter Six

Shortly before Christmas 1995, a box arrived from Smithfield. I had already sent a package to the house on Brogden Road: a small box that included a set of Monet note cards, a silk scarf that reminded me of the sea, and a framed photo of our children, *her* grandchildren. I knew so little about her and could only guess her likes and dislikes, what would bring a smile to her face.

I laughed when I saw the package was from Betsy, noticing that the pre-printed return address label was the same I had used in my mailing to her. The kind you get from charities that send Christmas cards and ask you to donate. We must be on the same mailing lists. Every connection counts.

Taking her box into the living room, I headed for our well-worn La-Z-Boy. How many hours had I spent in this chair, rocking babies, looking out the window at an enormous tulip tree, enjoying it in all seasons. I wondered if Elizabeth had a favorite chair—where it was placed in her living room and if I would ever get to see it.

I cradled her package in my arms for a long time. A package from my mother. I had no expectation of a gift from her, not even a Christmas gift. Even before opening it, it made the relationship seem more real. I almost didn't want to open it, didn't want to disturb the work of her hands that had prepared it for mailing.

"Mom, what's in the box?"

The chorus of children coming home from school prompted me to find scissors. Samson jumped up on the table to paw at the tape, her favorite plaything. Inside, nothing was wrapped. There were several boxes of pecans from her trees, two decks of cards, a box of stationery, a poinsettia brooch, and two lovely journals, one with a cover the shade of moss, the other a lavender blue. She had enclosed a card that wished us "Happy Holidays".

Dear Dianne and Family,

Sorry nothing is labeled. It's just a hodge-podge of little gifts for the whole family. I wish you all peace, joy, health and happiness and God's blessings now and always,

My love to all,

Elizabeth.

Tucked in a corner, protected by tissue paper, I found a Nancy Drew mystery - "The Clue in the Diary". *What a strange gift*, I thought. I mean, yes, I had loved Nancy Drew stories as a young girl—had collected most of them and passed them on to my daughters and now to my granddaughter. But this was definitely a new book, not handed down to anyone.

The front cover proclaimed "The Originals! Just as You Remember Them! With an introduction by Margaret Maron." Carefully opening its pages, I found this message:

My friend, Margaret Maron, who dedicated her introduction to the Nancy Drew book to me, lives on her family farm in Johnston County. She is the author of twelve mystery novels and numerous short stories published here and abroad. Her work has been nominated for every major award in the American mystery field. In 1993, her North Carolina-based "Bootleggers Daughter" won the Edgar Allen Poe award; the Anthony Award for the best mystery novel of the year; the Agatha Award for Best Traditional Novel. Her most recent novel, "Fugitive Colors", was published this spring by Mysterious Press along with the paperback edition of last year's "Shooting at Loons".

I slowly settled back into the La-Z-Boy and, with my sons as an audience, read each word aloud. The introduction was titled:

"Nancy, George and Miss Betsy Sanders"
By Margaret Maron

When I was a child, living on the eastern edge of our family farm, summertime seemed an endless round of chopping, picking, bending, weeding. Chores weren't something to keep a child out of mischief;

they were a necessary contribution to a farm family's well-being.

Nevertheless, everyone in our family read, and there were plenty of lazy Sunday afternoons or long summer evenings, after work was put aside and before sleep claimed us, when the whole farm seemed wreathed in silence. No television, no ringing phones. Telephone lines hadn't yet reached our part of Johnston County, and no one we knew owned a television. Radio was just past its prime in those days, and we usually turned it off after the evening newscast. Often, the only sounds that competed with our turning pages were night birds, cicadas, an occasional car bumping past on the dirt road in front of our house, and maybe the clink of ice in tall glasses of strong sweet tea.

We bought few books, and our periodicals were consumed the day they arrived: The Raleigh Times, of course; The Progressive Farmer; Reader's Digest; The Saturday Evening Post. These were my parents' staples and I would quickly thumb through them for the comics and cartoons. A neighbor used to pass his old Popular Mechanics magazines on to my older brother, and our mother would occasionally take "trial" subscriptions to Redbook, McCall's, or Ladies' Home Journal. (Regular subscriptions were deemed too expensive.)

But books we had – murder mysteries piled on the kitchen bench at my mother's place, humor and travel books strewn across my father's bedspread, adventures and fictionalized biographies stacked in a box on the floor beside my bed, even a handful of picture books on a high shelf within easy reach when we wanted to read to her but safe from the baby's sticky fingers.

So where did we get these riches?

We borrowed them from our county library. Or, to be precise, we borrowed them from the county's bookmobile.

Once a month, that great green box on wheels would come lumbering down our dusty road and, with a clash of gears, maneuver itself into the shade of my grandmother's crepe myrtle trees. No air conditioning, of course, but small windows could be cranked open for ventilation.

My cousin Nell and I would dart barefooted up the hot metal steps into the dim close interior and watch Miss Betsy Sanders pull books off the backward slanting shelves. Most of the books she recommended had boys as the main protagonists because, Miss Betsy said, shaking her head over such folly, "girls will read books about boys, but boys won't read books about girls."

To a ten-year old girl living in a Southern patriarchy, this seemed blatantly unfair since I didn't know any boys, not even my own brother, who would read any books unless they weren't forced to. But there was nothing to be gained by grumbling. I filled my box with as many books as I was allowed and hoped that there would be something interesting to swap with Nell or to sneak from Mother's stack when I'd devoured my own.

I was a voracious, indiscriminate, and totally non-judgmental reader who could suspend disbelief as soon as my eyes fell on the first line of the printed page. I cringe now to read the casual racist or anti-Semitic slurs contained in so many books written before World War II, but back then my eyes skipped over those phrases the way my mind skipped over prickly heat, mosquito bites, chiggers, or any other irritants that tried to get between me and the story itself.

The Nancy Drew adventures were my favorite, and I always read them first (and sometimes last, too, because I often reread books if that month's pickings had been slim). "The Hidden Staircase" was my introduction to the series, and, if memory serves, "The Clue in the Diary" was second. After that the order gets muddled. It never dawned on me that there was a sequence to the books or that I could have asked

Miss Betsy to bring me every Nancy Drew mystery in the Johnston County Library. Instead, it depended totally on the luck of the draw. Sometimes two months would go by without seeing a single Nancy Drew on the shelves; then, astonishingly, there would be four or five, and at least one of those would be an adventure I hadn't yet read.

Bliss!

But was it also cause and effect? Did my early reading of Nancy Drew turn me into a mystery novelist? Or was I drawn to those books because my mind already enjoyed riddles, secrets, and convoluted mazes?

When my colleagues and I compare our memories of Nancy, I'm amused that so many pictured themselves as that spunky motherless girl detective, dashing around the countryside in her blue roadster.

Not me. My mother was too real, my father too unindulgent, my days too full of structured obligations to put myself in Nancy Drew's stylish shoes and floor the gas pedal to freedom.

Tomboyish George Fayne was quite another matter though. Warm-hearted, loyal, practical, and supportive, George was every bit as interesting to me as Nancy herself. Clearly answerable to a vigilant mother and therefore unable to go adventuring every time Nancy beckoned, she was nevertheless less concerned with conventional feminine dress and conventional feminine propriety than either her cousin Bess or Nancy. Whenever I imagined myself into their world, it was as George.

Today, I look at the three friends and recognize that dainty, feminine Bess Marvin and sturdy, boyish George Fayne symbolize the two warring sides of female adolescence that must be integrated into a Nancy Drew wholeness.

Back then, as a self-conscious child who felt herself to be homely and inadequate, I admired

George's confidence and her determination not to be fettered by society's dicta of proper feminine behavior and appearance. (In a day when all pretty girls were supposed to have curly hair, it didn't seem to bother George one little bit that hers was as straight as mine!)

Bess was a wimp and Nancy played both sides so that she could be admired for both her courage and her femininity; but not only did George not seek approval and admiration, there were times when she actively thumbed her nose at it. Nancy Drew was perfection and I was willing to respect her accomplishments as much as George seemed to, but oh how I used to wish there were more of less-than-perfect George in each book.

Yes, Nancy Drew was a fine role model for young girls and I wouldn't take anything for the hours of pleasure those books gave me, but my image of her is inextricably bound up in my memory of the sturdy pragmatic woman who put her adventures into my hands.

Miss Betsy Sanders did not have curly, blonde hair, and she drove a cranky old worn-out bookmobile, not a sleek blue roadster. She had to earn her own living, not exist as the indulged daughter of a well-to-do-attorney. She wore tailored gabardine slacks at a time when most women wore flowery print dresses. If the bookmobile got a flat tire on some isolated back road, Miss Betsy changed it. When the radiator boiled over or the starter balked, she climbed under the hood and fixed it.

I wanted to be just like her.

Miss Betsy wasn't Nancy Drew all grown up. But I bet she was George.

What an astounding gift! Words written by a well-known mystery writer who had been influenced as a child by my mother, Johnston County's first bookmobile lady. My mother, who had taken a bus to Chicago and driven *that great green box on wheels* back to Johnston County;

who for years had brought the adventures of reading to small family farms—to families who otherwise would have had little access to books.

And now Margaret Maron had given me access to a dimension of my mother that I could never have had. She described my mother as "sturdy and pragmatic". A woman who was "self-sufficient and practical" and I found myself weighing her words against the woman who was in the process of revealing herself to me.

The front page, I noticed, was autographed.

Merry Christmas!
Margaret Maron
1995

Merry Christmas to you, as well, Ms. Maron. And thank you.

Chapter Seven

These thoughts crowd my memory as Aimee and I first enter Smithfield. Within this private reverie, I find comfort and much needed courage. It is April 19, 1997.

A year and a half has passed. A year and a half of phone calls and letters and pictures exchanged with a mother I call Elizabeth. And now they have brought me to the town of my ancestors. The town where I would have been raised had Elizabeth been able to keep me. A town where no one even knows I exist.

Driving through its quiet unassuming streets this April day, I savor its littleness, its almost deliberate understatement. I understand, even more fully, my mother's shock at being found and am awed by the miracle that she was.

The sign reads Main Street, and my eye immediately catches an arrow pointing to St. Ann's Catholic Church. My family's church, I knew.

"Turn here, Aimee," I say, and we detour to find it.

It is a tiny chapel of a church, blue-gray and trimmed in white. A circular stained glass window honors the Madonna and Child. Manicured flowerbeds surround it, and a white sign announces the schedule of Masses in both English and Spanish. I recall the picture my mother had sent me of herself, red hibiscus in hand, standing on the front steps of this very church, and I want to stand there, too. I look around for a red hibiscus but find none in bloom.

"Would you take my picture, please, Aimee," I ask as I place myself on the steps. *O holy place of family found.* I am deeply peaceful and leave with great reluctance.

Back on Main Street we are delighted by signs everywhere heralding the town's Ham 'N Yam Festival—a yearly event we find out. Streets cordoned off display booths filled with crafts, while games beckon the young and not so young. A country band gathers a crowd with foot-stomping, hand-clapping exuberance. Booths selling hot dogs and sweet potato fries, Smithfield ham dinners and bloomin' onions alternate with stands selling beer and soda and bubble gum the size of golf balls. We find a stage set up on the banks of the Neuse River where a young woman sings folk songs in a voice soprano, clear and true, her audience of ice-cream licking children playing tag on the hillside sloping to the stage. Aimee and I share a bloomin' onion while I keep looking for faces of the family who I am certain have been here often over the years. No one looks familiar, yet I am happy to be here, sharing in their common experience no matter where or when. For the moment, it is enough.

The singer is replaced by another with a voice not quite so clear, and I am restless. We retrace our steps to the car and ask directions to Brogden Road. Aimee takes the wheel, and we are soon on a two lane country road with houses fields apart. 2810 is the number we look for. 2810 Brogden Road. My mother's home. Until this second, only an address I penned to mail her letters.

"I live by myself," she had told me. "In the original family farmhouse." And then, it is there, before me.

Aimee slows to a stop, and all time is suspended. It is as if I have left my body and hover over the place where my mother lives. In my mind's eye I am walking the land inch by inch. Deliberately. Slowly. Absorbing fully its flavor. I want Elizabeth to come to the door and greet me and take me by the hand. I want her to show me every flower planted, name every tree, point out the pecan orchard and the scarred earth where the holly tree fell during Hurricane Francis last fall. I want us to meander through the fields together, wander back to the pond where picnics gathered friends and family over all these years, while I picnicked on Northern shores with my other family, unaware of my Southern roots. I want to look for the white deer Elizabeth told me she sees from her back porch window, who comes to enjoy the salt lick. I know there is a small statue of St. Francis in the yard out back, too, welcoming, protecting all the wild things.

Show me St. Francis, Elizabeth, and introduce me to all the creatures large and small that visit your land. Show me. Embrace me. Be with me.

But the time isn't right, and I am still in the car, driving slowly past this place where my mother lives. It seems to me so dear, yet so careworn, in need of loving attention. It sits closer to the road than I thought it would, with tulips and daffodils near the end of their blooming, framing the porch. It reminds me of the family plantation home in Tennessee Williams' "Cat on a Hot Tin Roof". My mother's house, with its sloping tin roof sheltering the upstairs veranda. My mother's house, so Southern, so foreign. And I am so drawn to its fading grandeur.

The name Sanders is painted in black letters on her battered mailbox. And as we continue down Brogden Road, we find another house and then another, with that same name on their mailboxes, and I know we are seeing the places where uncles and aunts and cousins *live and move and have their being.*

"Drive past Elizabeth's house again, Aimee," I ask. And again and again, until common sense returns and we wend our way wordlessly back to the center of town.

We find a place to spend the night and order dinner in a tiny cafe named Monet. Aimee eats with great appetite, her own meal and part of my own. I tuck my girl safely in our motel room and return to Brogden Road alone. It is now 8 o'clock.

Chapter Eight

A lifetime to be here...

A calm descends upon me as I leave the parking lot of the Knight's Inn. Calmer than any calm I have known. I am home. In the town of my ancestors. The place of my "begats". The thought reverberates inside of me until my entire self is a smile. *Brogden Road here I come!* I cheer myself on, and the smile becomes a grin.

With a deliberate slowness uncharacteristic of my Northern bent, I find my way to the house at 2810, carefully following its outline with hungry eyes, reassuring myself that it is still there. Just beyond the house, on the other side of the road, a long driveway leads deep into the fields to a tiny church, complete with steeple and a very small parking lot. Here I pause. Breathing deeply, I stretch my legs, surveying my kingdom. Everything is still. *Only me and the sky and an old whippoorwill*—remnants of a favorite childhood melody flow from my memory, and I find myself humming.

I am in a state of consciousness new to me, moving on a level of discernment where every breath is perfectly synchronized with every other breath: every fiber, every cell moving as one. Elizabeth doesn't know I am in Smithfield. On Brogden Road. So close. I close my eyes and pray for both of us.

"Yes, I would like to meet you," she has said. And I knew she meant it. "But no one knows about you." This filled her with great anxiety, and she had canceled our meeting twice. "My nephew and his family are coming for a visit," she had cautioned one time. A hospital stay postponed another planned visit, deepening my resolve to meet her soon. This time would be different. This time, fear would have no chance to play a role.

Dark clouds threaten to unleash rivers of rain, then change their mind, absorbed in the blackness. Cicadas whine about me in sound-surround, and creatures unknown rustle in the fields. Voices, rising and falling in the distance, bring comfort and a sense of normalcy to a situation that is far from normal.

I stand for a while by the edge of the road, listening to my own inner voice. I listen as the Hale-Bopp comet flickers overhead. I listen as a car passes by with unseemly speed. I listen in stillness, until the message comes, bubbling forth from my very core, permeating every cell of blood and bone.

"It is time," self says to self.

I walk back to my car.

Near the end of the road is a service station with a public telephone. With no trace of the calm that had been my reality such a short time ago, I dial her number.

"Hello." Her familiar voice answers.

"It's Dianne," I say, barely able to articulate even my name.

"What's wrong, Darlin'," she says, her concern evident. "It's okay, just spit it out."

"What's wrong. What's wrong," I say, stammering, "is that I'm on Brogden Road."

"On Brogden! Where on Brogden?"

"At the service station."

"Well," she says in front of a long pause. "Come on down!"

"Yes!" I shout. I cannot help myself. I am jubilant. I am going to see my mother. *Yes!*

"Just give me ten minutes to get ready," Elizabeth's voice seems to smile.

Ten minutes. Ten eternal minutes. And without warning, tears come soundlessly, streaming from places hidden and secret.

Chapter Nine

In ten minutes exactly I turn into her driveway, every breath, every movement in slow motion. "I'll be at the front door," she said. I step out of the car, walking over rough and uneven ground, up the front step to the well-lit porch.

"Have I come to the right place?" I say.

"Yes, this is the right place." She greets me in a sweater of deepest red, worn with black tailored slacks, a black medallion bearing an Indian design her only decoration. Her short white hair is freshly combed. This touches me so, and I feel at once her dignity and her vulnerability. Her small features are softened in a smile so dear it crinkles her face, inviting me in.

Shoulder to shoulder we stand. Touching. I slip my arm behind her waist.

"You are so beautiful," I say, those words repeating in my mind.

Her mother-voice calms me. "You are beautiful too."

"Where shall we visit?" I ask, whispering, as if I am in a church or a library. I feel my body swaying in harmony with my deepest self as we move as one into her gracious living room.

"Well, we could visit here" she says with a lilt to her voice, "Or we could visit in the kitchen over a glass of wine."

Perfect, I think, nodding.

"No matter where I greet my guests," she says, "they always love my kitchen best." And with quiet grace, she leads the way.

We enter a room which is small and cluttered, warmed by a space heater tucked into a corner. An old black telephone shares space with a twenty-inch television on the back wall counter. Stacks of letters and books and a mug filled with pencils and pens sits on a modest wooden table painted white. A soft pillow straddles one chair.

"Here's where I do most everythin'," she explains. "Eat, write, watch TV, read."

Two wine glasses sit among the dishes drying in a white drainer near the sink. One glass is exquisitely cut. The other, plain. I watch as she carefully places the beautifully cut glass on the counter and rummages through her cupboard until she finds a matching glass. She fills them both from a bottle of Grenache.

"To us," she says, proposing a toast.

"To us."

"Are you ok?" I ask as we take our places across from one another at the small wooden table.

"I'm numb," she says.

"I'm just so glad you said I could come."

"I could never refuse you."

My mother's words bring quick tears to my eyes.

"I never dreamed this would be happenin'," she says, "but it is."

She takes a sip of wine.

"I always knew you were out there somewhere," she says. "Hoped and prayed you had a good life, and now I can see that you did."

There is silence then, an uncomfortable silence. We stumble about for words, feeling awkward, ungainly. There are no rituals, no instructions for such a meeting, and I feel all instincts leave me.

In a musing voice, Elizabeth begins to speak, her Southern accent sweeping over me.

"I went to a funeral yesterday. A friend, ninety-three years old, and thank the Lord she died because she was already gone. There were three priests on the altar, and that made me think of my own funeral and how many priests there would be. And what they would *think* of me if this were ever revealed. All the esteem, all I've worked so hard for..."

Her voice trails off, and I feel so bad for her suffering—and for my own. And for all the injustices and misunderstandings that make it awkward for us, mother and daughter, to be together. In a rush of words, I assure her I will never reveal to anyone in Smithfield who I am, that I always have and always will, respect her privacy—that she is the one in charge.

"Please feel safe," I say and I want to put my arms around her. And with that flood of necessary and heart-felt words, I know I have given away any chance of ever knowing the rest of my family and a quick pang of sadness sweeps through me. Still, there is no way I can do anything that would hurt this woman of eighty-three years. This mother-woman. I feel so protective of her. Elizabeth, who is so brave, so very dear.

"I appreciate that," she says and visibly relaxes.

"Are you ready to see some pictures now?" She goes to an adjoining room, a room cluttered and crowded, filled with precariously stacked boxes, and albums piled high. A room filled with the scent of must and dusty dark bookcases and intricate dressers begging to be explored. Here treasures lay, and she brings forth photographs and mementos, and we relax together, skimming the ages. The pictures, a perfect vehicle to share family history. Stories about her mother and daddy, family friends and her particular friends, sisters, brothers, their children and children's children. Only one of her sisters and one brother are still living. Susan Barbour, her youngest sister, and Bill Sanders who both have homes on Brogden Road, one on each side of her own. With each word, each picture, each turn of the page, my sense of family deepens.

"Do any of these faces seem familiar?" she asks. "Do they remind you at all of your children?"

I love that question.

"Yes," I reply with great happiness. "Many seem familiar. Especially this group of pictures. This one child in particular reminds me of my daughter, Aimee, the one who is with me."

"That is the daughter of my sister, Alice," she says. "Alice married a St. Peter, and they had ten children."

It is now after eleven o'clock, and we stop for a break.

"Are you tired?" I ask.

She looks at the clock. "Not midnight yet!" She laughs. "But I do have to be in bed by twelve so I can get up for the eight o'clock Mass."

I tell her we had found St. Ann's and ask if she would feel safe if Aimee and I went there to a later Mass.

"There is an eleven o'clock Mass," she says, then pauses. "But why don't you come to the eight o'clock?"

I am incredulous. "But isn't that the Mass that Susan and Bill and some of their families go to?"

She nods, looking almost mischievous, conspiratorial. "I think we can handle it. Don't you?"

I look at her with wonder and delight, loving this surprising and courageous lady more with each breath.

"My daughter, Aimee, will be with me. Is that all right?"

"Of course, that's how I'll meet her." Her reply left no doubt that she was in charge.

"I'll greet you outside the Church, "she says, "and introduce you as travelers coming through and tell the family you are going to join us for breakfast."

For breakfast, she said! Join the family for breakfast!

"Susan knows about you." Her tone more serious. "I told her soon after you first contacted me. I figured *someone* ought to know about you in case something happened to me."

I feel exhilarated. I want to squeeze her and jump about in a most primitive kind of joy-filled dance.

I exist. She said so out loud, to her closest friend, to her sister, to Susan, my namesake!

And now she's letting that other one see me. Meet me. I can only stutter in amazement and blurt out the first thing that comes to me.

"What did Susan say?" I want to know.

"Well, her *first* words were… 'and Mother never knew?'" She laughs softly. She thinks for a moment then says, "I won't tell Susan who you are until after you've gone. Oh, wait, but Susan knows your name," she suddenly remembers, "and will recognize you from the pictures you sent me."

I fear she will change her mind and quickly offer to change my name.

"I can be anybody," I say.

"No," she says. "You just be Dianne. Everything will be all right."

It is time to go. She takes me on a tour through the downstairs, stopping first to look at each portrait placed lovingly in what Elizabeth calls *The Gallery*. Mother. Daddy. Each of their children. Groupings of grandchildren. All are memorialized in ornate frames. An oil painting of a uniformed naval officer holds center stage in the living room.

"An ancestor?" I ask.

It is, she tells me, but I am too saturated to absorb any more information and stop listening.

She shows me a splendid bedroom filled with Victorian furniture from an aunt long deceased. Then leads me to her own room, so strikingly modest and spare. A single bed, carefully made. A single dresser. A crucifix on the wall. An unpretentious area rug perfectly centered on the dark wooden floor. Two single windows look out on spacious fields.

We walk through an enclosed porch filled with shelving laden with jars and displays of shells and stones. An antique dressing table holds a low, flat bowl, overflowing with myriad shapes and kinds of arrowheads and broken pieces of pottery.

"Found on the land," she says. Intuiting my need for connection to the land itself, she carefully selects seven of the arrowheads and places them into my hands.

"For my grandchildren," she whispers with tenderness.

We move to the dining room where she shows me an artist's rendition of her home.

"A friend presented this to me on my seventy-fifth birthday," she tells me. I remember then that I have my camera with me, and ask if I might take her picture standing by this painting. She graciously assents, and I wish that somehow I could have a picture of both of us together.

As we walk back through the living room, she stops to take a picture out of a frame. A photograph of herself with Susan and Bill sitting around a picnic table.

"Would you like to have this?" she asks in her unassuming way. I take it from her outstretched hand, feeling myself drawn even more closely into the circle that is family.

We are by the front door now. I put everything I am carrying down on a nearby table: camera, arrowheads, pictures. We hold each other gently. A quiet hug. I could have stood there forever.

I step off the porch onto the ground where the holly tree lost in Hurricane Francis once offered her shade. I open the door to my car, blow her a kiss, and drive away.

It is just past midnight when I reach the motel. Aimee unchains the door. Words tumble effortlessly as I tell her about my evening—tell her about her *grandmother*. I sleep soundly then, lulled by the sweetness of my mother's love.

Chapter Ten

Sunday, 6 A.M. A day already sun-filled. It seems to me a hallowed day. A day of promise. And something more than promise. Deeper. Richer.

My senses are taut with anticipation and such overwhelming happiness, I can't help but hug myself. I think of my mother's hug, gentle and tender and warm. I feel its imprint even now. I think of it as an indelible sign. An invisible pressure marking me as hers.

I reach over and touch my own child's face, restful and serene in sleep. I want to fold her in my arms, passing on to her my mother's hug. I wonder how she will feel as she meets her grandmother for the first time.

"I'm really happy for you, Mom," she has told me. "Because I know how important this is for you, but it really doesn't affect me at all." I can only smile at such sweet naïveté.

A slow stretching shower brings freshness to my limbs, and I let the water pour over me for a very long time, sensing in the waters' flow a kind of baptism.

I am a Sanders, and this morning I will be among my own people, in the Church where they have worshipped for generations. In the Church my great-grandparents helped build.

I dress with care but am dissatisfied, wondering why I packed all the wrong clothes. A sweater from Aimee's suitcase rescues me. Unruly hair finally tamed, I awaken Aimee who readies herself effortlessly. With a final check around the room, we gather our belongings and go to our car.

The way to St. Ann's already memorized, we are there in minutes. We park across the street and walk slowly to the entrance of the church.

The atmosphere is electric, charged with a surreal quality. It is as if I am now living in the flesh what has always been a shadow-land. I wonder if Elizabeth feels this same sense of unreality.

We are greeted outside the doors of St. Ann's by a scruffy-looking priest and a rather portly woman. She hands us a bulletin, and then we are inside.

Light filters softly through stained glass windows, casting bluish tones on whitewashed walls. Folding chairs sit behind well-worn pews to accommodate the overflow. We stand here for a moment, unsure. I am acutely aware that Elizabeth has not yet arrived.

There is but a single aisle in this tiny church, with pews on either side. Each pew seating four people comfortably.

"Follow me," I whisper to Aimee. I begin walking tentatively toward the altar, taking the first space for two available. I kneel automatically and take a quick breath. It is Susan who sits directly in front of me. My mother's sister. The aunt for whom I am named. I recognize her from the pictures and, transfixed by the force of her presence, cannot take my eyes from her slender form.

She is taller than I expected, straight and strong in appearance. Her attire is tasteful: classic beige slacks and a white sweater, as white as her short bobbed hair. She wears glasses and is in quiet conversation with a much shorter woman seated next to her. I speculate about this other, younger woman, with clear, smooth skin and short, dark curls. She, too, wears glasses. A small gold pin, a replica of a lizard, decorates her navy blue tailored outfit.

To the right and closer to the altar, I recognize Elizabeth's brother Bill, who towers over those around him. As Susan stands tallest of those around her. As I stand taller than those near me. *My people are tall people.* The thought somehow grounds me, as if my own sixty-nine inches suddenly makes sense.

My attention is drawn to the back of the church as I hear the voice of my mother exchanging good-mornings with the greeter, and I am filled with a sense of relief.

She's here, my mother is here! I sing to myself. Tension ebbs as I let go of the fear that she may have changed her mind or, even worse, that I may have caused her to suffer a heart attack.

The Mass begins, and my attention turns to the altar. The priest's gestures are open and inclusive. His homily, mercifully short. The celebration continues its familiar pace. The Creed. The Prayer of the Faithful. The Consecration.

At the Sign of Peace, I watch fascinated as Susan hugs the woman next to her, then turns to shake first my hand then Aimee's in that simple gesture of good will. I wonder what Elizabeth thinks as she sees us make this ritualistic connection.

Susan reaches back to hug the woman next to me, and I am startled to think that this unknown lady, too, is most likely family. I am standing next to family, with family in front of me and behind me. *Touching* family. Blood family with whom I share a genealogy. A family tree *real*, not borrowed. Its impact is beyond thinking, beyond feeling.

Communion. Post Communion. And then the Mass is ended.

"Go forth in peace," says the priest.

We walk out of St. Anne's, Aimee and I. There to the right of the wooden steps, my mother stands, just as she had said she would. She appears composed, quiet, wearing a black blazer over a blouse with blue and beige-toned swirls. A blouse I recognize from her family's formal portrait.

She takes my hand in greeting and then, with an expression of untold tenderness, places her hands over Aimee's own, gently taking her grandchild into her heart.

Susan walks towards us then. Aunt Susan and two others. Elizabeth greets them, and in her soft, Southern voice, introduces us.

"This is Dianne Riordan and her daughter, Aimee," she says. "They are travelin' through and will be joinin' us for breakfast." Then she turns to us.

"My sister, Susan Barbour."

"Oh!" says Susan, knowing instantly who we are. And without missing a beat, she extends her hand in welcome and introduces us to the women with her.

"My daughter, Jessie and my daughter, Frankie."

Jessie had been sitting next to Susan; Frankie next to me. *So this is Frankie*, I think. Frankie, who lives next door to my mother. And Jessie, who I knew had just moved back to Smithfield from Charlotte. Robert, Susan's oldest son, also joins us.

Frankie uses her expressive hands to tell us to "follow the brigade" to McDonald's where the family gathers for breakfast most Sunday mornings.

How strange that this most memorable event should take place in a setting as innocuous as McDonald's. Yet it seems to me wonderfully appropriate, too. A faceless background, familiar and unobtrusive. The focus not food, but family.

Chapter Eleven

There is a long line at McDonald's. Only one cook is on duty and one lone young man to take orders. Everyone is patient. Our group is cheerful and animated. I listen, fascinated by the laconic dialogue between Susan and her daughters, Frankie happily explaining the references to names and places unknown to us, their northern guests.

Elizabeth orders coffee and a single muffin. She will not let me pay for her. Aimee's order and my own quickly follow, and the three of us take our seats in a booth near Susan's family. I sit next to Elizabeth, and Aimee sits directly across from her.

The green-blue eyes of my mother peer into the green-blue eyes of her grandchild. Feasting on eyes that match. Eyes that are set closer together than mine. Her grandmother's eyes.

We sit in silence. In deepening quietude. Even our words seem silent. Aimee speaks of her students and of what it is like to be a new teacher, in a new city and state. Elizabeth places her hands on the table. She leans forward as if she cannot bear to miss a single word. Her face rapt in attention.

"She's lovely," Elizabeth whispers to me.

"Like her grandmother," I whisper back.

Susan and company leave first, exchanging pleasantries.

"Nice meetin' you. Drive safely," they say. But as Susan passes our table, she places her hand on my shoulder, a caress that bade me welcome more than a thousand words.

"Time to get ready for Frankie's birthday party." Elizabeth's softly spoken words indicate that it is time for us to leave also.

Bill and his family exit the restaurant at the same time, and after another round of introductions, Bill walks with us to Elizabeth's car.

"Betsy," he remarks casually to his sister. "Doesn't this young lady remind you of Theresa?"

"She does indeed." Elizabeth nods, her face turning toward her grandchild.

"Theresa is our niece," Bill explains. "One of our sister Alice's ten children. The resemblance is striking."

I watch Aimee receive this information. She holds it closely, not daring to reply. Bill helps my mother into her vintage black station wagon, and I feel a sense of dread, of emptiness spill over me. She is leaving. My mother is leaving. And I can't even hug her.

"Thank you for your wonderful hospitality." The only words I can manage.

"Have a safe trip," she says to us, her voice barely audible.

The car door swings closed. Dumbstruck, I watch as she drives away.

Bill is with us still. I find myself thinking how much he reminds me of Fran, our oldest son. The way his hair waves back from his forehead is familiar as is the way he stands—relaxed and easy in his movement. Gracious and outgoing, he accompanies us to our car, chatting amiably about life in Johnston County, offering us vignettes about his first car, stories about his mother and daddy, and what it was like growing up with five sisters. I absorb every word, each syllable rounding out my history. I feel as if I have known this kind man all my life.

Once more goodbyes are said. Bill tells us to please stop and visit any time we might be passing through.

"We will," I promise.

It does not seem possible to just drive away, but that is exactly what we do.

It is a three and a half hour drive to Aimee's home in Charlotte.

"I loved meeting Elizabeth, Mom," her voice nudging me from my reverie. "I'm so happy to be a part of her. Part of *all* of them. They're such fine people."

I call Elizabeth that night. The night after the McDonald's breakfast. The night after I watched her drive away.

"How are you doing?" I ask. "Are you okay?"

"I'm very okay," she answers. "I'm very pleased with the way things worked out."

Her answer, so simply phrased, makes me smile. I am still full of the drama of all that happened and can hardly begin to put it into perspective.

"Tell me what Susan said."

And without hesitation, my mother relayed Susan's words.

"They have seen the faces of the family, and that can only be good."

Profound words, it seems to me. Down to earth. Drawn from the wealth of a life lived rooted in people and place. Spoken to Elizabeth as the family gathered for Frankie's fortieth birthday. We talk only a few minutes more when my mother passed on my cousin Robert's remarks.

"Aunt Betsy," he'd said. "Those women who joined us for breakfast. I've seen them before. They've been at St. Ann's before. I'm sure of it."

Chapter Twelve

All the yesterdays I have lived
Today are coming together.
All the tears I have shed,
All the joyous time
And the bad times
All moments
Are leading to this
A new beginning.

I cannot stop thinking about who I am. Who I *really* am. I am Dianne. Wife of Frank. Mother of seven. Raised a member of the Flore clan with names like Phelan and Blatner and Hassenfrantz and Boyle. Lynch, Froment and Democioux. French names, Irish names and German—all part of my borrowed heritage.

"My relatives are from Alsace-Lorraine," I used to say. "And Tipperary, Ireland. And from a small town just outside of Paris."

I loved saying the names aloud, wrapping my tongue around each syllable. Glad to have such words in my family tree, borrowed or not. Legitimate words. Legitimate names. Somehow they seemed to make *me* legitimate. Real by association, as it were.

I borrowed their stories, too. The story of how Uncle Edward became the first president of the Bartenders Association of America and an advisor to President Roosevelt. And how Aunt Bertha led the first Suffragists Parade down Buffalo's Main Street.

But most of all, it pleased me to take on the simple "how they met" stories that led to the marriages forming their family trees.

I loved knowing that my grandmother on my mother Helen's side was a nurse in St. Catharines, Ontario, who met my grandfather on a visit to a cousin who lived in Hamburg, New York. Kathleen and Charles settled in Buffalo and had seven children. Helen, second-born, became my adopted mother at the age of thirty-three.

Isabelle Froment, grandmother on my father's side, met William Charles Flore at a dance on the Crystal Beach boat, even though he didn't like to dance. Despite this flaw, they married and had but one child, a son, William George, who became my adopted dad.

Isabelle's sisters were Anna, Louise and Eugenie, all born in France. Anna wrote for the society page of *The Courier Express*, Buffalo, New York's only morning newspaper at the time, and traveled to places that seemed exotic to me, like Toronto and Manhattan. I got to wear a gypsy costume that was a relic from her travels when I was a child on Halloween.

When I knew her, she was white-haired and tiny, and we visited her on the second floor of a brownstone building in a bohemian part of the city. I loved her apartment and used to pretend it was in the heart of Paris and that I was a mysterious Parisian.

Ari was their only brother. A romantic name I thought. A cabinet maker, Uncle Ari's hands were always stained a deep brownish-red. He carved the molds for the animals that flank the entrances to the Buffalo Zoo. It was fun having bragging rights to such an uncle.

Louise married someone of whom I have no memory. Eugenie married Harry Ehmke and lived in a white farmhouse in Silver Creek, New York, which was just far enough away to be an adventure. I loved our visits to this farm. Its barns and land and gardens were magical. There was always a new calf to love and lots of kittens and cats. Flowers grew wildly. There were arrowheads to find, streams and ponds to explore, haystacks to climb.

But it was the house itself that drew me, that filled my being with quiet content. The veranda facing Main Street with its comfortable rockers of white wicker. The old-fashioned parlor and dining room with wide-planked floors and faded flowered carpets. White laced doilies under every lamp; books spilling everywhere and jars of coins in unpredictable places. And a huge kitchen with a white iron stove. Cousins named Tehkla and Curtis and Basil added to the enchantment of those visits, and I left each time with the greatest reluctance.

The Democioux's, my Grandmother Flore's cousins, also had a farm and a wonderful old farmhouse, theirs in Eden, New York. This was a real working farm with crops to harvest and cows to milk. Those dear ladies never failed to offer me, a city child, the separated cream, still warm from milking. Our last ritual was a stroll in their garden. Here they would help me pick the biggest possible bouquet—so big I could hardly reach my arms around the stems. I felt like royalty and buried my face in fragrant petals of roses and chrysanthemums and daisies all the way home.

My grandparents took me on many outings over the years, but none touched my child-soul as deeply as our visits to those two wonderful farms. I've often thought that maybe, somewhere deep within, the child that I was, carried within her the memory of that original family farm-house lived in by my mother, Elizabeth. Maybe I carried the sounds and the knowing of that life before birth, beyond memory, and so was able to recognize in the deepest part of me, that sense of being truly at home on a farm.

I am Dianne. Raised a Flore. With Flore memories. And relations. And a cottage in Canada as part of my story. And camps and Camp Fire Girl meetings and two brothers, Bill and Gene, and a sister, Kathleen—all younger.

Yet at this point in my history, all that seems the shadow part. The *found* part of me, the me named Susanne, recognizes the reality of all of my past, its concreteness, its place in my journey. But how do I wed the two? The Flore part and the Sanders part.

I am no longer separated from my past, that veiled mystery that held me captive. Yet I *was* separated. For over fifty years. Separated from my mother who carried me within. Separated from all that bound me to myself—my roots, my very heritage. Separated, I could not know who I was, and so I write to bring all the parts of me together. To make sense of all my history. To tread without fear with steps firmly planted on fixed earth. Hiding from no one. And from no experience.

I hid myself in all those experiences of growing up. Hid in all the good things as well as things not so good. I wanted to hide the very truth of my life: that I was adopted. For me it was a forbidden word. Full of pain, and sadness. And yes, shame.

Yet, Helen and Bill were truly Mom and Dad. They gave me what was theirs to give. They gave me their identity. And they gave unstintingly and without question.

Helen had four aunts to give and two uncles plus their spouses and twenty-two first cousins as well. I was fourth oldest of all the cousins and loved my place in the family's order. I loved *my family*, and especially our gatherings on Easter and on Christmas Day at Aunt Agnes' home where Grandma Blatner lived. And Thanksgiving always happening at our house. A sit-down affair with tables everywhere. It was my job to make place cards and decide the seating arrangements for over forty people. Oh how I relished that power.

Our summer place was Long Beach, Ontario. Here my aunts and uncles and cousins would come each Sunday, spilling out of cars crammed with towels and picnic baskets and inflatable rafts all making a beeline for the beach. I couldn't wait for those wonder-filled Sundays.

Yet even here, in this most sacred of family havens where all should feel safe and protected. Even here—one day I was no longer safe.

My cousin who was fifth in line, angry at me for some reason long forgotten, said to cousins two and three, "We don't have to play with Dianne. After all, she's not our *real* cousin."

And so I, unreal cousin, left. And was not missed by anyone.

My mother left. My first mother, Elizabeth.

I came into the world with a flattened head, and scratches on my face. One ear stuck out. She saw me from the nursery window. Just once. And then no more. If I had been perfect in appearance, without the punishing marks of a forceps birth, would she have been so quick to leave? Maybe she would have lingered with me awhile. Maybe even hold me or croon in my ear. Maybe her scent would have sustained me all those years. Maybe...

But I am learning her story. And I know the whys. And I love her fiercely, this wonderful, reluctant mother of mine.

Growing up, I never told anyone that I was adopted. Not my friends, not even my best friends. Nor did I talk about it with my brothers and sister. Nor was it mentioned in my presence anywhere in the family. But when I found my mother Elizabeth, I shouted her presence to the whole world. There is nothing like being real.

Betsy - 1942

Helen with Dianne

Dianne Sanders Riordan

Mom & Dad with Kathleen, Dianne (standing) and Billy

Dianne (left) with brother Gene and sister Kathleen

The family farmhouse - 2810 Brogden Road

Growing up in Buffalo, NY

Betsy, center. Left to right are Aunt Susan, Uncle Bill and Aunt Martha

St. Ann's

Dianne and Frank

Betsy's grandchildren! Left to right - Matthew, Fran,
Chris. Standing - Tim, Danielle, Erika, Aimee

3 generations: Standing - Cassie with Trent, Erika, Dianne, Kerry, Aimee with Bryce, Jess with Vera. Seated: Fran with Sadie and Brooke, Tim with Finn, Frank, Keith with Alexandra, Chris. Matt and Emilie are in the foreground.

Scott, Danielle and Andrew live in Tacoma, WA

Greg, Christian and Nathan - Erika's sons.

Betsy and Dianne - 1997.

On Brogden Road with cousins Helen, Jessie and Aunt Susan.
Standing: Cousins Bill Joe, Sarah, Robin, Patsy, Jenny.

Chapter Thirteen

January 23, 1997 marks Aimee's twenty-sixth birthday. My plan is to fly to Charlotte to celebrate her day. And celebrate we do. Only this time I have a second agenda. A mission of sorts.

On previous visits to North Carolina, I would borrow Aimee's car and drive to Smithfield to visit Elizabeth. It is a journey of three and a half hours, and I always drove back that same evening. Not this time though. This time I am determined to spend the night. At my mother's house, that is. Not that I've ever been invited to do so—nor have I been invited this time. It's just that it is something I need to do. I have no plan, no idea how this will happen. Simply a knowing that it will. I am painfully aware that for Elizabeth, fear continues to be present—fear of someone finding out I am her daughter. My promise to keep her safe, her only security.

It is stormy that day.

"Rainin' cats and dogs," Elizabeth puts it. The rain is falling in sheets, thunderous on the old tin roof. "I love that sound," she says. "Brings back childhood memories... 'specially summertime rains. There's no insulation in this old house, so the noise pounded over our heads somethin' fierce. I'd always come downstairs and run to one of the out-buildings to watch the fireworks. Usually one of the Airedales would follow me and we'd cuddle, so to speak—so close both of us could stay warm."

I love how she lapses into stories, each one rounding out my sense of who she is. Who I am.

Night is falling quickly, the sense of darkness heightened by the storm's unrelenting downpour. The sky is electric and branches from the holly tree tap the windows. I feel safe. Protected within the walls of the family farmhouse. Marble table tops hold Tiffany style lamps radiating golden halos all around us. We are cocooned in a velvety room of overstuffed chairs and sofas draped with afghans. Just my mother and me.

"I wonder if it's storming in Charlotte," I muse aloud. "I'd better call Aimee and let her know my plans."

I dial slowly, and after five rings reach her answering machine. "I'll be on my way soon," I say, projecting clearly, well within Elizabeth's hearing.

"Not tonight you won't," her voice booms.

"No?" I say, trying to keep the smile from my voice. "Where will I stay then?"

I want to remember how the worn planks felt beneath my feet that night—the first time I slept on Brogden Road. The first time in oh, so many visits. Invited this night. No, commanded. My mother's voice imperious.

"You will spend the night here," her words determined. "In the bed your grandmother inherited from her aunt in Raleigh."

The room is crowded with sturdy, age-worn furniture. A huge wardrobe fills one corner. An imposing chest of drawers stands flush against the wall next to the four-poster bed. Its frame sits high and is covered by a heavy, hand-stitched quilt of soft cream with green vines and pale blooms of blue and yellow.

The walls are a faded peach, soot-stained around the small fireplace opposite the bed. Two windows slant recklessly on either side, white paint peeling in ragged curls. This is the guest room. The room my cousins claim on their visits. Unmet cousins whose pictures I have memorized. Whose names are imprinted in my heart:

Bill Joe. Laura Jean. Theresa. Mary. Patsy. Sarah.

Tonight I stake my claim. My right to this room of my ancestors. I want to carve my initials boldly on the immense double door frame marking the entrance. A rite of passage. An exclamation point of ownership. D.S.R. - for Dianne Sanders Riordan I would carve. Or maybe simply S.S. – Susanne Sanders. The name on my *real* birth certificate. The name that gives me access.

I fold back the quilt and pause, my gaze resting on each object. Photographs of family lining the mantle, knickknacks of frogs, shells in decorative jars, a picture of the child Jesus framed in ivory, a crucifix next to the wardrobe. A heavy layer of dust has settled over everything, and I remember Elizabeth's smiling assessment of herself.

"Never did take to housework," she had told me in her no nonsense way. "Too busy findin' things to do outside. 'Twasn't mechanical, either. Daddy wouldn't even let me milk the cows! Said he couldn't afford to feed the ground."

Slowly, a sense of reverence directing my movements, I sit down on the bed, finding comfort in its firmness. My feet are bare, dangling freely over the side. Slipping down onto the floor, I stand still, taking in the sensations of being in the middle of history. Family history.

"This old house embraces me every time I walk through its door," I heard Aunt Susan once say. And now it is my turn to be embraced.

My feet absorb its energy first, a radiant warmth seeping into me. I begin to slide across the floor, unwilling to lift my feet. I slide through the house. Through the hallway, living room, dining room, kitchen. I shuffle up the stairs to the second floor and back down again. Giddy with belonging. With being invited. With being a Sanders.

Returning to the guest room I stand solid. My legs are pillars. Strong. Strengthened and upheld by generations before me. Strengthened by an awareness of the tongue-in-groove connectedness to all the trials and all the joys of those who have tread this ground before me. Holy ground. With prayers of thanksgiving filling my pores, I lie down beneath the quilt, beneath sheets smelling faintly of lavender and dust. Sleep comes quickly when you are home.

"Dianne. Dianne." I wake to the sound of my mother calling me. "Thought you'd be awake before me," she complains with a smile. "I've made us oatmeal."

Chapter Fourteen

The soil is loamy, rich and black as a night sky naked of stars. Sweat and dirt cake my arms and face, and my cutoff jeans and baggy t-shirt are way beyond respectability. The garden is my playground, and I am so at home weeding its overgrown beds. It is mid-August. Black-eyed Susans have overtaken one whole corner of the bed surrounding the deck. Gladiolas have ceased their blooming, and the impatiens are overlapping mounds of color. Tomatoes bow to the earth, globes of red and almost red whispering secrets to the marigolds gathered around them because, someone once told me, they keep the weevils at bay.

I am a simple gardener. I love the lushness of it all and relish the layers of color and scent. But today I am thinking of my mother's garden, its haphazard mishmash of color spilling everywhere. I see it plainly, my mother meandering its paths. Ancient crepe myrtles raining blossoms of silk, their trunks twisted with hidden wisdom. Cicadas scraping their backs against the gnarly trunks, safely shedding outgrown shells. Bearded irises, once reigning proudly along the gravel driveway, are being choked out by thick bladed monkey grass. Orange and yellow day lilies loudly compete with orange and yellow bushes of lantana. Pink trumpeted four o'clocks, hydrangeas, hardy larkspur and waves of pink and white phlox keep the dilapidated barn feeling young. Morning glories catch hold of a small fence out back while verbena dance along the ground. Clay pots filled with petunias overflow the steps to her front porch while a red hibiscus startles the eye with its perfection.

"I'm a mud putterer," she so colorfully puts it as she talks about her garden. "I'm always amazed at what pops up year after year, just for my enjoyment." I love this about her. Her spontaneity reflected everywhere, indoors and out. And I take after her, I think. Even though there are all those years of not knowing her, not knowing her likes or dislikes, her passions, her dreams. Yes, I take after her. Imagine that. Oh how my musings please me, and I hug them close smudging more dirt on cheek and brow.

"I'm like my mama, my mama's like me." Happy, I belt out a parody of the old fashioned tune, "I love my baby, my baby loves me". I am amazed at how much I am learning from her even as I learn about her. I wish my life were simpler so I could go and be by her side for long periods of time. *Be with me, Mama,* I think. *For many more years. Come and see my garden fair, and both of us together can get our hands and knees muddy. And delight in earthworms and spiders and the ebb and flow of seasons.*

"It's your Aunt Susan," Frank calls from the screened-in porch, breaking my reverie. And when I pick up the phone, I know from the sound of her greeting that she has nothing good to tell me.

"Your mother is very ill." My aunt's slow drawl chills me. "She was taken by ambulance to the emergency room and admitted immediately. She is havin' so much trouble with her breathin'. The doctor says it's critical."

Without thought, I throw essentials into a small overnight bag and, with a kiss to my husband, enter the twilight zone of unknowing. Not knowing how I will be able to drive the seven hundred and fifty-eight miles to Smithfield by myself. Not knowing if Elizabeth will still be alive when I reach her. I gather strength, remembering my mother's stories of driving by herself to Chicago to gather nieces and nephews to spend their summers under her wing in the southern place of their roots. My mind playing one refrain only. *Hang on, Mama. Don't leave me.* A mantra prayed in concert with the humming of tires traveling highways at breakneck speed.

It is late when I arrive in Smithfield, the parking lot at Johnston Memorial Hospital almost empty. There is no one to question me as I walk through the front door and head for the elevator. Room 207, Aunt Susan had said.

A quarantine sign jolts me. A cart with a supply of masks and gowns and gloves stands as a sentinel outside her door. Do not enter without protective covering, without checking at the nurses' station, it warns.

Instinctively I follow directions and put on the mask and gown required. I feel like a space alien and experience a momentary fear of being discovered. Fear of someone questioning my right to be there. After all, only "next of kin" are usually acknowledged as ones who have access to the very ill. And I, though daughter, am still unacknowledged to all but Aunt Susan. I am one without status, without rights. With great trepidation, I open the door. Elizabeth, Miss Betsy, is lying on her right side, her left arm, horribly bruised, lies still across her hip. Only the hiss of oxygen assures me she is alive. Never have I been in the presence of anyone more frail, more ill.

Leaning against the bars of her bed, I begin my vigil, my breath in sync with her breath as if willing her breathing to become less labored, less forced. It is just after 10 o'clock.

"Have you seen Susan yet?" Elizabeth's eyes flutter open and then close again. "You'd better call and let her know you've arrived safely," her words whispery, barely discernible. "They've given me a sleepin' pill, so you'd best get some rest yourself. I'll still be here in the mornin', I promise." Each sentence spoken with effort as she moves in and out of consciousness.

I drive to the house at 2810 Brogden Road, a mere ten minutes from the hospital, down that long, two-lane rural road, over the railroad tracks, past an entrance to the I-95 on its way to Florida. I pass the gas station where I once made that heart-stopping phone call now over three years ago. The call that let her know I was just down the road, on the night I first saw her face to face. Aunt Susan lives there now, as well as Betsy. She has temporarily moved there from her home across the street to care for my mother. I feel awkward. Out of place. Without bearings. This is my mother's home, the family homestead, but my mother is not here. Aunt Susan, though gracious, still seems to me a stranger. She does belong here. It had been her growing up place.

"Would you like a glass of wine?" she invites kindly.

And I follow her to the kitchen as I had once followed my mother.

"It doesn't look good," Susan begins, her hands tightly folded. "The doctors don't know how she has hung on this long. Betsy yelled at me when I said you were comin'. Said she wished you wouldn't."

Her words stun me like a slap, and my tongue feels claustrophobic. Such power in secrets. My head understands Betsy's fear, her difficulty in not knowing how to explain my presence to whoever might walk into her hospital room. Yet my whole being rages against such fear. How can it be possible that a mother dying would be afraid of her daughter being by her side? So deeply afraid someone will find out that once upon a time, over fifty years ago, a child was born. Born and surrendered. Because that's the way it was. Because an unmarried daughter couldn't bring home a baby. Because she would be disowned. And bring disgrace upon her family. Upon herself. And her child.

"The hardest thing was givin' birth—you were the first grandchild born in the family—and not being able to bring you home to Mother.

To leave you behind and carry on as if nothin' had happened. And that's what I did. Nothing else was possible."

These words spoken tremulously during one of our first phone calls. Those phone calls where I found out that, for the first three years of my life, Betsy and I lived but a mile from one another. Knowing that the one mile might as well have been a million. Even now, with death so imminent, shame and guilt and an inordinate fear of exposure are present. A force as powerful as it is unreasonable and I am helpless to overcome it.

"Be at peace, Mama," I pray earnestly. "I won't let anything happen to you. I won't give away your secret. You are safe with me. You are safe."

I toss restlessly in her bed that night, choking on nightmares that toss me angrily into a netherworld of derision and disgrace and shame.

Chapter Fifteen

I awake to the filtered light of early morning sun. Blue birds and finches and chickadees are already enjoying the welcoming mix of sunflower seeds and suet. To experience the sound and sight of chattering birds as my mother experiences it brings a happy ache to my chest. I make a note to make sure all the feeders are full before I leave.

I approach her hospital room gingerly, putting on the required mask and gown. Her breathing seems easier to me, and my own breathing relaxes. As if sensing my presence, a smile touches her dry, whitened lips.

"Did you sleep well?" she whispers.

And I report on what birds came to visit outside her window this morning, knowing this will please her.

Interrupted and unsettled sleeping plagues her morning. Nurses and aides march purposefully in and out, recording vitals, and fluid intake and output and all those things deemed necessary by hospitals. No one questions my presence. One young nurse asks if I am Miss Betsy's daughter, and Betsy's long drawn out "Yes" thrills my ears and heart.

"How did she know that?" Betsy questions pensively as the pleasant and efficient young woman closed the door behind her.

"Maybe we look alike," I tease, hoping she doesn't become agitated.

Everything seems in slow motion, the hours suspended. Her small voice interrupts the silence. "Kindly bring me my journal, and open it to last Sunday."

Though so terribly weak, there is no question that she is in charge. Her journal is small, only 3 inches by 5, with no adornment of any kind. Each page accommodates four dated entries.

"Write 'admitted to the hospital'," she orders. "And under today, write 'Dianne came'. We'll have to wait and see what happens next."

She thanks me and admonishes me to be sure and put the journal back so it doesn't get misplaced. And I wonder how a woman who has spent her entire life among books, this once- upon-a-time Book Mobile lady, can use so few words to chronicle her life. More poignantly than ever, I realize how little I know this mother before me. My sadness intensifies knowing there is so little time left.

Aunt Susan arrives and invites me to take a break.

"Walk yourself to the cafeteria or go outside before the heat gets too strong," she urges. And I do.

When I return Aunt Susan is waiting for me outside Betsy's room.

"The doctor came while you were gone." She speaks slowly, in the matter of fact tone of one who has witnessed more than her share of suffering and death. "She's failin' quickly and there's not much to be done. Not much she *wants* to have done besides bein' givin' oxygen and medication so she won't be in pain. She's ready to die, she has told me, and she asked me to tell you to please go to the house and take anything you might want—for remembrance sake."

But there's nothing for me to want. Not at the house. I only want more time with her. To know her better. To be acknowledged to the family. To be a part of them, too. But that's not to be. Betsy is kind, but dismissive. I stay only because I cannot bear to go. It is as if I am in a fight for my life too, and I am losing.

It is nearing midnight, and it's clear that I must leave. Kneeling next to her, I trace the sign of the cross on her forehead, lightly feathering her hair from her brow. Her hot, pale face is tissue thin, and I place my own cool face next to hers. She is my mother, and I don't know how to say goodbye.

"Drive safe, darlin'," she says with eyes not quite open. "I love you."

"I love you, too." In tender silence I add the word, *Mama*. A word I can't quite say aloud. No one has given me permission. Not even myself.

Chapter Sixteen

Daylight is waning as I begin the trek home, my heart heavy with a sense of endings. "Home is where one starts from…" T. S. Eliot wrote. And here is my starting place: this small, nondescript village in the world of the rural South. But how can you start from some place when you aren't even supposed to *be?*

Reality presses heavily on my shoulders. Reality extinguishing all of my fairy tales. Dreams of Elizabeth graciously presenting me to my family.

"This is my daughter," she would say, her voice low, shy with perhaps a hint of surprised pride. And to me, "Meet your family." And aunts and uncles and cousins of all degrees would crowd about me, and I would be folded in their welcoming hugs. But Elizabeth is dying. And there is no more time.

The play of clouds moving across the sun diverts my attention. A performance of color and light, spreading a raiment of hues over the *mackerel sky*—an Elizabeth expression, I remember. Soon it will rain.

The sounds and sights of the countryside quickly recede as I drive North, the I-95 stretching monotonously, hypnotically before me. My mind a movie reel, set on rewind, accompanies the drone of wheels. Remembrances of visits and phone calls; the excitement of letters; remembering the cadence of her sprawling speech—all propel me beyond my heaviness.

My mind settles on an earlier visit, almost a year earlier. It is late March. My visit a stop-over on our way to Fort Myers Beach, Florida—a yearly trek for spring training. Our son's spring training, not professional spring training—practical field practice for Chris's varsity baseball team. My husband is with me, and Matthew, our youngest.

Elizabeth is once again in Johnston Memorial Hospital, and I visit her alone that night, my husband and son firmly settled in the nearby Hampton Inn with pizza and a movie suitable for a twelve year old.

I find the hospital with ease and walk unchallenged into her private room. Elizabeth is resting on her side, white, wavy hair flattened against the pillow. A medal of the Blessed Mother is tangled around the oxygen paraphernalia.

"Been waitin' for you," she smiles.

I bend to kiss her, and her lips feel sweet and moist.

"This is the first time I've ever driven thirteen hours just to visit someone in the hospital," I tease. Her forehead, dry and hot, surprises my touch. Both of her arms are bruised.

"They keep punchin' me with needles," she complains, following my gaze. "This medicine in one arm, another in the other. Always had good veins before now, veins that bulged out before they even tightened the rope, so to speak."

"So do I," I jump in, glad to find any connection with this found mother, even bulging veins.

I find her unusually talkative this night and pull my chair close. I lean forward to be even closer. I want to feel her breath mingle with my breath as we try to find what is lost, hold sacred what is found. I savor this moment of intimacy, knowing our moments together must be enough. Knowing they will never be enough.

She tells me that her sister Susan went to a wake that day—a friend of theirs from the Coast had died. Margaret. I listen carefully, absorbing her descriptive phrasing, her quiet drawl still slightly foreign to my Northern ear.

"A real fireball she was," she says. "Nothin' daunted her! She just tackled life with gusto. But then she began to experience pains in her back and hip, and no one could pinpoint it til it was too late. The doctor gave her six months. She only had two. We were such good friends, and I wasn't able to visit her..." Her voice trembles with traces of unshed tears.

"So death has been a bit on my mind and makin' me a bit sad. But not really. Especially Margaret. She was completely bedridden. Had such pain. She was only seventy."

She asks me to bring her the obituary page, carefully folded on the shelf by the dresser. She is animated by words too long pent up.

"Another friend of mine is written up here, too," she tells me. "A monsignor. Another independent type, feisty and fun lovin'. One day, shortly after you found me, he said to me, 'Well, Betsy, at least we never contributed to the population explosion!' Imagine what he'd think if he knew about you! Of course, he got the lion's share of the obituary page. Two whole columns!"

New glimpses of my mother's world expand my own, and I listen even more carefully. Her voice continues, tinged by a far away quality of remembering. "The monsignor who died... he knew I had applied for a dispensation to marry Kenneth, your father, but I never went through with it. I found out later that things could have worked out, but by then Kenneth was gone. And then, so was I..."

She pauses, sighing deeply, her words falling like water on gravel.

"He wanted us to get married, Kenneth did. He didn't want you given up for adoption."

A nurse enters peremptorily and busies herself about Miss Betsy's room. Professionally checking pulse and temperature, importantly recording numbers on a chart. I can't wait for her to leave. I have questions to ask that I had never thought to ask. Never dreamed I would have the chance, or if the chance, the courage. Her words are piercing, each syllable hammering my flesh. She seems not to notice and continues. A relentless monologue of memory. I hardly dare breathe.

"I always wondered if Mother knew," she says. "The excuse I gave for going north was so flimsy."

I am parched, drained by the heat of the room, by the fire of my own emotions. I sip from a cup of tepid water sitting on the dull metal tray next to her bed. I want to offer her a sip as well but want nothing to interrupt the flow of her words.

"I told Mama that someone who lived on Euclid Avenue in Buffalo, New York, told Father Higgins, he was a friend who told me about the home for unwed mothers in Buffalo, that there were employment opportunities because of the War and that I was going to go there and get a job. She never questioned me."

And I know, with deep certainty, that she had wanted her mother to question her.

"So I took a train and a taxi and presented myself at the home," Betsy continues. "Father Baker's, they called it. There was an openin' in the kitchen, and I asked if I could take it. I worked there til I left, sometime in October."

I breathe my questions with an anxiety that almost force the words from my mouth.

"Did you ever see me after I was born? Did you ever hold me?"

My need to know is suddenly urgent. Crucial. My very understanding of myself at stake.

Her faded blue eyes hold mine. She speaks deliberately, carefully choosing her words.

"You were a hard birth," she began. "I labored a day and a half til they put me out. I lost a lot of blood. Next day they told me I had delivered a girl. They had to use forceps so you were quite marked up.

"I went by the nursery only once. And then no more. And no, I never held you. Couldn't bring myself to do that. It was too hard. So I simply abandoned you."

I am listening now as if this were someone else's story. I am both my mother and the babe in the nursery. I sense my grandmother there, too. Listening. Knowing.

"I remember one of the girls who kept her child askin' 'why doesn't Betsy ever see her babe?' I never could bring myself to answer. I was just always thankful I never had to work in the nursery. Soon as I was able, I went back to my job in the kitchen where I stayed til I was strong enough to leave.

"I always thought the babies knew. Babies cried when I held them. I always thought they cried for you. And no one ever asked me to babysit."

With each word, Elizabeth's voice grows fainter. Though I sense her exhaustion, I press her further.

"But what about Susan's children?" I ask. "Aunt Susan has told me she never could have managed without your help raising her children."

"But not until they were *children*," she explains. "When I could do things with them, and teach them things. And bring them to the coast with me. Yes, Susan's children have childhood memories of growing up with me. And my sister, Alice's children, too—bringin' them back to Smithfield from Chicago each summer. So we could know them…"

But what about knowing me? the child in me cried.

Chapter Seventeen

Home again, I am reabsorbed by things familiar. Husband and children and the routine of my work all help keep me grounded, attuned to the present. Thoughts of Elizabeth accompany my every step.

I find it hard to share my sadness even with those closest to me—to say out loud, *my mother is dying*. My mother, Helen, my other mother, sweet adoptive mother, has already died. Was mourned, waked and buried. Friends and family shared my grief. Understood my pain and stood with me. But I have two mothers. And today the weight is heavy.

My mother is dying. And she doesn't want me to be there. She chided Aunt Susan for letting me know. Was relieved when I left. And now I am left, feeling lost and desolate.

Time is a haze as I wait for news—news of her death, of funeral arrangements, date and time. I've told Aunt Susan that I want to come to Smithfield when Betsy dies. I want to be present at her wake, be at her funeral. I want to hear what people say—let their words carry me and give me insight.

"You don't have to let anyone know who I am," I assure her. And she promises to inform me.

Her call comes late one evening and leaves me reeling—tossed by emotions I can't even grasp. The reality of Susan's words incomprehensible.

"Your mother is holdin' court with all your cousins," she relates, her voice calm and matter-of-fact. And I know they have come from Jacksonville and Greensboro, Nashville and New Jersey to say goodbye, summoned by Elizabeth, herself.

"The nurse offered to take a broom and sweep them all out," she says. "But she was havin' too grand a time and told her to go away!"

My cousins summoned while I, like the nurse, am sent away. The message clear. I am in a twilight zone filled with ambiguity. A sense of outrage and anger, helplessness and sadness compete and overtake my sanity. I manage to thank Susan for calling, feeling foolish and invisible and oh, so devastated.

Memories swirl and I relive the moments I first spoke to my mother, first heard her voice.

"I have always prayed for you," Elizabeth told me during our first phone call so long ago.

Pray for us sinners, now and at the hour of our death. The familiar words of the Hail Mary begin to play in my mind like a mantra bringing me solace. I pray for my mother. I pray for me. There is nothing else.

A second call comes days later. Another report from Susan. A report both unexpected and astounding.

"The doctor told your mother that she is no longer dyin' and that he needed to reinsert her feedin' tube. Betsy agreed, as long as she could go home. I'll be movin' into the old house to care for her. My daughter Sarah has been stayin' with Betsy off and on, so between the two of us and the visitin' nurses, we'll do just fine. She'll be discharged on Sunday."

And with this news, tension ebbs, and I breathe deeply, as if for the very first time.

Sunday Elizabeth will go home. My mother still with me. Nothing else matters. And hope returns.

I call a florist and order roses. Tea roses. Tiny buds of muted pink. Her favorite, she had once told me. I listened carefully to all her favorites, wanting to please her. Wanting to know her. Knowing that, in knowing her, I'm knowing me. Puzzled, because tea roses aren't my favorite and muted pink is much too tame to be at home with me.

I decide to send her not a bouquet, but a narrow planter, just wide enough to be placed on the generous white window sills of her nineteenth century farmhouse. I wonder where she will place it, and hope she will choose the window by her bed. I sign the card *Dianne*—nothing more—and am startled by the anonymity of it all.

It is Sunday, and I can't wait to call. I can feel the words forming on my lips, delicious words, fresh like moist dew.

"Good morning, Elizabeth," I sing. Her voice though, is subdued, and I am brought to the reality of how ill she has been, how frail she is still. She says she is glad to be going home and our conversation is filled with the lightness of small talk. She never mentions my gift, and I ask her if she received anything from me. It is out of character for me to ask, but I can't help myself. I want her to know how much I celebrate her, celebrate that she is my mother. Her "yes" is spoken quietly, drawn out in many syllables as if to buy time.

"I wish you wouldn't send me things" she blurts out, frustrated. "It's too hard to explain!"

I promise not to send her any more gifts.

And so Elizabeth returns to 2810 Brogden Road. Aunt Susan and Sarah take up residence there. Doctors and nurses, pulmonary specialists, relatives, friends all coming and going. My phone calls to her are abbreviated, cut short by her discomfort that someone might ask questions. Might wonder who is calling.

It is three years and eight months since our first contact. And over these short years I have seen the faces of many members of the family, heard their voices, even been introduced to some of them. But not as myself. Never as myself except to Aunt Susan. Only as Dianne. Someone she met. Someone passing through. I am grateful for what has been freely given. I will let that be enough.

> *Dear Aunt Susan,*
>
> *I am writing to let you know that I am backing out of the picture. Not giving up, but letting go. It seems to me that Elizabeth needs all her strength just to get through each day. Her distress about my calling, about the possibility of questions being asked, drains her of energy, and I can't bear to cause her pain or conflict. I love her deeply and am so grateful she received me—grateful for her embrace of all my family. I am grateful for the sharing of memories, so important to both of us I think.*
>
> *I want her to rest easy, knowing that all is well and all shall be well. But if, dear Susan, you think I am wrong in my assessment of how things are, or if you sense a shift, or if she tells you she wants to hear from me, or to even see me—I am here.*
>
> *I send you my love,*
>
> *Dianne*

I seal the letter and mail it with a sense of closure. I can no longer bridge the gap. I can no longer be an embarrassment. It is enough.

Chapter Eighteen

"One of the luminous things about adoption is that
its mystery holds the possibility for miracles."

Journey of the Adopted Self, Betty Jean Lifton

I am at peace. A resigned peace. I have let Betsy go. Let my mother go. Up until this moment, I have been the director and principal actress of my own play. And I am tired.

It was I who searched for Betsy. I who phoned her and intruded myself into her comfortably constructed life. The life she created as *Miss Betsy*. She was the matriarch. Pillar of her beloved parish, St. Ann's. Maiden aunt. Bookmobile lady. Member of the Ladies' Guild. Nature lover. Gatekeeper of the family home. Gardener. Collector of frogs and seashells.

It was I who kept calling. Wondering with each call if she really wanted to hear from me, knowing she would be too curious not to answer, too polite to hang up. Each call becoming a stretch—for me, yes, and for her as well.

Through these calls I learned the rhythm of her life, the pattern of her thoughts, the idiosyncrasies of her speech. I learned she was a night owl and that her brother Bill was too. And that he often called or stopped by when all was quiet.

"He's good company, and I get a lot of one-on-one time, then." And I could tell how pleased she was.

It was I who came to Smithfield. Again and again and again. Manufacturing reasons. Any reason. We might be on our way to and from Florida, and after all, Smithfield is just off the I-95. Or visiting Aimee in

Charlotte, and oh, how about if I stop by for the day. It's only a three and a half hour drive. Or, we are in Greensboro, North Carolina for a baseball scouting trip for our son Chris, then a senior in high school. Fran, captain of his baseball team at Allegany College, is with us, too, scoping out the competition for his younger brother.

"What a great chance to meet your grandsons!" I had said. *That* visit, one of my sweetest memories. It was September 20, 1998.

She was expecting us, sitting by the fireplace, erect, dressed elegantly in a silky white blouse. A royal blue scarf draped her shoulders. Her dappled hand rested on a cane, and I wondered how long she had been there, waiting. My usually easy-going boys were tongue-tied by her presence.

Her greeting was quiet. All of us stumbling for words. For normalcy. How do you introduce grandchildren to their grandmother? A grandmother to her grandchildren?

"Would you care to show the boys through the house before we go out?" she offered, breaking the awkwardness. I am startled by her offering. To show my sons the family home—this home of my ancestors, and theirs as well. It felt like a sacred trust. A precious gift of recognition and belonging.

An unexpected joy welled up within me as I took my boys through the house. We roamed the rooms, the hallways; roamed the backyard that opens to fields of soy and beyond that to woodlands. We parted the heavy damask curtain that hid the steep staircase that led to the rooms on the second floor. Here, an enormous wardrobe dominated the bedroom, beckoning my sons to open its solid door.

"Narnia!" exclaims Chris.

Indeed, Narnia. And that sense of Narnia, of adventure and transformation carried us through the rest of that dear visit.

We dined at a restaurant of Betsy's choosing. And it was Betsy who directed our conversation, asking the boys about their lives, about baseball and school and if they had girlfriends. We skipped easily and lightly over various topics, listening, laughing. Dipping and diving into episodes and chapters of our daily lives. Sharing. A wonderful sharing.

And then back to Brogden Road for dessert of ice cream and cookies and Betsy delighting in displaying her collection of frogs. How she laughed when she startled Fran and Chris with a jumping frog that shouted, "Ribbit! Ribbit!" How playful and relaxed she became.

Yes, I am at peace. I know who I am. My memories sustain me.

Chapter Nineteen

One day in the fall of '99, an ordinary October day, less than two months after I sent Aunt Susan the letter, I picked up the phone. Susan was on the other end of the line.

"Well, the secret has been broken," Aunt Susan exclaimed. "Betsy has told Jessie about you. She gave me a way to tell Jessie, and then Jessie went to see her. I let the two of them have at it. Both of them were very much at peace when I came back."

How do you receive news that seems like a miracle? News relayed to me with Aunt Susan's matter-of-fact way of speaking. My mother, stubborn and stuck in fifty some years of silence, now chooses to share her secret—to share *me*—to acknowledge that she even *had* a daughter, to Susan's daughter, Jessie—her niece. Jessie, who just over thirty years ago also gave birth to a daughter. And like Betsy, surrendered her daughter to adoption.

"Would it have helped if you had known about me?" asks Betsy of Jessie.

"Of course it would have, Aunt Betsy," acknowledges Jess. "But I am grateful to know even now. I am so happy that you have met *your* daughter, to know that I have another cousin."

Jessie's warmth reassures her, giving her courage and peace and yes, happiness.

A flurry of letters flow back and forth following this breaking news.

Dear Jessie,

I've started to write you a million times but have no words. I can't wait to be with you. Your phone call after talking to Betsy was such a gift to me.

Time is moving at a snail's pace. Is the weekend of October 29th okay with you?

Love,

Your cousin Dianne

—

My dearest mother,

You are the most surprising lady! A lady of courage and great heart. I cannot even begin to tell you how much it means to me that you shared our story with Jessie. I wish I were free enough to hop on a plane and knock on your door right now! I want to be sure you don't get cold feet!

Do you think my cousins will remember me from the McDonald's breakfast? Do you think they will see a resemblance to you or to the family?

I am filled with such anticipation. But strangely, there is a deep calm within me. It feels as if all is happening just as it should. Unfolding in an order somehow pre-ordained. Do you feel this way?

Stay at peace, dear one. I am coming.

Love,

Dianne

—

Susan's oldest child, Ann Nolan, married to Shane and living in New Jersey, reached out to me as well.

Dear Cousin,

When I heard that you are coming to Smithfield this weekend, I arranged my plans so I could visit at the same time. I so very much look forward to meeting you and welcoming you into the family.

As Aunt Betsy's niece, I am so glad to have this opportunity to see another side of her. She is a wonderful aunt. Without her, I would not have experienced a side of life outside the farm.

I think Jessie let you know our cousin, Bill Joe, is also coming up to Smithfield from Florida this weekend.

With warmest welcome and regards,

Ann Nolan

Chapter Twenty

October 29, 1999 arrives quietly. Without fanfare of any kind. It is a cloudless day filled with the warmth of the sun's rays that seem to dance before me as I pull into the gravel driveway of my mother's home.

Bill Joe St. Peter is the first to greet me. He is standing near the beloved crepe myrtle by the sloping front porch of the old farmhouse. He stomps out his cigarette and walks slowly to meet me.

"So, we're cousins," he says, echoing the words he first said to Betsy when she let him know about me. "So, you're a mother," he had said to her. And I remember her telling me how his down-to-earth acceptance had given her great comfort.

"Everyone has been so supportive," she said over and over again, surprise continually overtaking her.

Bill Joe's eyes smile. He is tall and thin and has a studious look about him despite the jeans and t-shirt. I know he is an engineer. I know he is married to Robin and has two children, Keith and Laura.

"Yes, we are cousins. First cousins!" Because degrees are important, especially in the South. "I believe I am the oldest cousin," I say with a grin—because rank is important as well. I am amazed at how comfortable I feel. Even gracious, as if I were the hostess and he the visitor.

Bill Joe and I walk to the backyard where my mother is waiting. She sits at ease in an Adirondack style chair, wearing a floppy, aqua hat to protect her from the sun. Her eyes crinkle in greeting as I bend to hug her. She seems so tiny, this mother, who once matched my own five feet nine inches. A mint green sweater accents the narrowness of her shoulders.

Others have already gathered. Aunt Susan, Jessie, Ann, Sarah, Gina, Frankie, her husband, Bill. Uncle Bill and his wife, Ruth stop over as well as Will, Jr. and his wife Debra. People I had met in passing on my many trips to Smithfield—and to whom I'd been introduced as Betsy's *friend*. What joy to be able to be here as myself. I want to hold hands with everyone and dance a circle dance and maybe do a handstand or two. *I'm me*, I want to shout, *and I belong here*. But I don't have to shout because no one is questioning me. No one.

My memories of that visit are warm and nourishing. So many expressions of welcome. Betsy leans forward as we share stories and recipes and pictures. We even exclaim about the likeness of our toes and several of us stand with our feet next to one another for a picture.

"Royal toes," Elizabeth pronounces of the middle two toes somewhat joined together.

I feel Betsy's gaze holding me softly as I interact with the clan. I hope she feels as cared for as I do.

It is hard falling asleep that night. Hard to leave Betsy's side, even to say goodnight. She walks me to the foot of the stairs that leads to the room where the wardrobe to Narnia resides. We linger a bit and kiss each other's forehead in a kind of blessing.

I climb into the high four-poster bed and stretch myself between clean white sheets. I breathe in the scent of family, of Pond's moisturizing cream, of something faintly medicinal and musty. Everything feels just right.

We have only *partially* "come out", I learned at that gathering on Brogden Road. Betsy is still in the process of letting the rest of the family and her friends know about us. And that is okay with me. It is her territory. Her decision. It is a beginning.

The years before coming to Smithfield as *myself*—as Betsy's daughter—had been challenging. A Lenten time of flickering hope. A time to be melted and molded. A time of opening up to the dark and growing in trust. A time to learn how to receive as well as give. A time of great listening and deep self-knowing. A time spent waiting to be called by name so that I could answer.

Now that time is over. Dianne/Susanne are no longer separate, no longer canceling each other out. I am visible, and all is well.

Chapter Twenty-One

January 23, 2000 arrives crisp with the sharp bite of winter. I hadn't thought to check the weather in North Carolina, but I was heading *south* after all! Not only did I look forward to a break in the weather, but I was happy to be sharing in the celebration of Aimee's birthday and looking forward to a visit with Elizabeth.

The flight from Buffalo to Charlotte traversed a barren, monochrome sky of gray. As we neared Charlotte, grays turned to silver and white, and we landed in a city cloaked in a blanket of snow and ice. An unprepared Charlotte caught in a heavy snowstorm.

The drive to Smithfield becomes a harrowing experience over treacherous, untreated highways, and I arrive exhausted yet exhilarated from the challenge.

Entering the unlocked doors of the hospital, I take the elevator to the third floor and easily find my way to Elizabeth's room.

"I'd had some pain and some breathin' problems which I didn't like," she had told me over the phone, "and so I finally consented to allow Susan to bring me to the hospital. They've been vacuumin' my lungs, and so I guess I'll have to stay awhile."

She is lying on her right side, and I can tell she is asleep. It is past eleven; the drive, an easy three and a half hours under normal conditions, had taken me well over six. The light by her bed is still on, and I know she had been waiting for me, unwilling to settle in for the night until I arrived.

I tiptoe to her bedside to turn out the light.

"Hey," she murmurs sleepily. "I'm so glad to see you. Thought you might not come because of the weather."

Smiling, I kiss her, pulling up a chair. Her face felt warm.

I tell her of my adventurous trip. How Highway 85 was at a standstill and about taking the 77 instead, of spinning out of control on Highway 40—spinning backward on black ice with no time to react.

"I spun across four lanes and onto the median where my car came to a complete stop, on the very edge of that median and facing the right way. I sat for a moment in real gratitude."

I speak quietly, surprised at the calmness I had felt. "Then I simply turned the car back on and edged cautiously back onto the highway."

"Your guardian angel must have taken over the wheel," she says, and I agree.

As we speak, I lean over and cover her left shoulder.

"I always feel so comforted when I'm covered like that," she says. "Thank you. The strangest thing has been happenin'." She reaches out to take my hand. "Sometimes, late at night, when everyone's asleep, I'll waken and feel a bit chilled, wishin' I could pull the covers up. And on several occasions, I'll sense a presence and feel the blanket placed gently over my shoulder. Like you just did. It never startles me. It just makes me feel warm and comfortable, and I snuggle up and go back to sleep. It happened again last night."

She drifts off to sleep, and I drift over to my cousin Jessie's house where I am spending the night. She welcomes me with a cup of hot chocolate and leads me to my bed.

We are awakened at eight the next morning by the phone.

"That was your mother," Jessie informs me. "Givin' orders. Wants her pillow and some other personals like Kleenex and shampoo. Doesn't want to have the hospital charge her for things she can bring from home. Told her her insurance covers such stuff, but she'll have none of it!"

Aunt Susan joins us for breakfast. Croissants and silken chocolate peanut butter, with coffee, hot and strong. These Sanders women know how to live right. It is wonderful to be with them—to be *one* with them.

Jessie had already de-iced my car and has it warmed for me. I gather my mother's "personals" and return to the hospital.

"I seem to have a frog in my throat that I can't put in my collection." she says by way of greeting. She loses no time introducing me to the day nurse, and I enjoy their playful interaction, my mother laughing as Sherri called her a "senile old woman" because she couldn't remember if Sherri had given her her morning nourishment. We laughed so hard.

The day passes quickly. In the afternoon her doctor comes in. A young woman probably in her thirties. Betsy introduces me as a person very dear to her who came in from Buffalo to visit. The doctor is very affectionate toward my mother and kisses her before she leaves.

"First time I've ever had a doctor who kissed me," she says.

I simply wish she had introduced me as her daughter.

"Would you tell me a bit more about Kenneth," I ask tentatively. She had told me the bare-bones of my story. But I want more, much more. She hesitates, and I pull my chair as close to her as possible. I don't want to miss even one word.

"Well," she says, "we met at a pub at Fort Bragg. I think I told you that. And we hit it off right away and he asked if he could walk me home. And we kept meetin' and goin' out. At that time I'd bring a lot of fellows home for the weekend, and Daddy would bring home a few strays he'd run into in town.

"Sometimes the boys would spend more time with Mama and Daddy, 'specially Daddy, fixin' cars and farm machinery while us girls would be waitin' and waitin', anxious to go into town, to a coffee shop or what have you. Daddy would keep the plates filled with fried chicken or whatever else Mama was cookin'. I think they were tryin' to find a husband for me. But somehow, I never had a strong desire to be married. I guess I didn't want to play second fiddle to anyone's job or anything else.

"I had a few proposals but always said no, until Kenneth. He was fun and easy to be with, and when he asked me to marry him, I said yes. And then Pearl Harbor happened, and the entire Ninth Division was going to be shipped out, first of all to Louisiana, and we went to a motel, and I guess we got carried away. And then I found out I was pregnant." Her voice dropped a bit and her eyes dropped too. I moved even closer, placing my hand over her hand. Her words gathered strength.

"So I went to my priest, Father Higgins, and started gathering all the paperwork necessary. Birth certificates and everything. And that's when I found out he had been married before.

"He told me that the marriage hadn't been anything more than a lark—they'd all been out drinkin' and someone suggested he and his date get married. And so they did. It didn't last long.

"But I couldn't marry a divorced man. Mama and Daddy would have been devastated and probably disown me. So I broke the engagement. Kenneth was inconsolable. He knew I was pregnant, and he wanted his child. Wanted me. But I said goodbye. The Ninth Division left. I never heard from him again."

She is still then. We both are. Lost in the story.

"I don't think Mother was too disappointed. She only commented that he had a weak chin. I was glad none of your children got that." She looks up at me then, searching. "But I always thought he was good-lookin'. His eyes were nice, and he had high cheek bones and nice teeth and hair. I don't even have a picture of him.

"I went to Buffalo in May and in September had a baby girl. Had you." She pauses for a moment. "I had such mixed emotions—"

The phone rings then. A loud, interfering ring. Betsy's friend Beulah. And after that, another friend called. And the story was broken.

Jessie arrives soon after, bringing my suitcase with her. She urges me to get on the road. "The temperature is droppin' and ice is formin' quickly."

Betsy looks out the window, delighting in the snow. "White caps on the bushes!" she says then urges me to be on my way as well. "Give my love to Aimee and to all your dear family."

"I love you to pieces," I say, and then, because I can't help it: "Aren't you glad we found each other?"

"I am," she says. "Yes, I am."

I call her when I reach Charlotte.

"I have a question I want to ask you," she says. "When my nurse Sherri, came in after you left she said, 'I'm so glad I was able to meet your daughter', and I wondered how she knew? It's okay, but I was just wondering."

"But I had said nothing to her about anything," I tell her quietly.

"I didn't think so, but I was curious. I told her a little bit about our story. She was glad for us."

Chapter Twenty-Two

In March of 2000, my mother died. On that day the sun shone dimly in a sky white-washed and gray. I wondered why it shone at all.

The morning had been so ordinary. An ordinary day filled with ordinary sounds. Steam chattering through the radiators. The cadence of children getting ready for school. Then the telephone rang and my cousin's words, muffled and halting, changed everything.

"This is hard," she says. "And I'm tryin' not to lose it. Your mama. She's dyin'. She wants you to come."

And so it is that grief formally inserts itself into my days and hours, announced by Sarah Birdsong, her voice choppy in distress, pulling me through the phone lines to a hospital bed seven hundred miles away. It slips between the pages of my normal life. Between dreaming of spring planting and getting ready for the St. Patrick's Day Parade. Between making dinners and the homeliness of laundry. Between the daily trek to work and the daily routine of errands.

Without warning, remnants of a phone call of just over a year ago rip through me.

—

"I'm gardenin'," Betsy had said. Her voice breathy, words separated by deep sighs. "Pullin' weeds to make room for lettuce and onions and some garlic, too, though I don't 'spect much will last the ravages of critters." Life breathing in, breathing out. The whistle of oxygen in the background reminding me of her frailness. "Lots of rabbits hoppin' about this yard," she continued. "Need a dog to scare them away. Didn't have to worry so much while my Airedales were with me."

In her world, pussy willows had already bloomed against hedges of honeysuckle. But here in our Buffalo suburb, snow lingered. While her earth was already pliable, mine was packed hard.

"I'm still perusing seed catalogs," I had told her.

A longing had filled me then. A longing to be with her, to kneel beside her as she tilled the soil, to take the trowel from her arthritic hands. I wanted her to direct me, tell me what to plant where and what to add to the soil to nourish the young seedlings. I had so much to learn from her

—

Fours hours later, I drive to the airport.

Clouds form low in the sky as my Southwest Airlines flight arcs toward Raleigh-Durham, swirling thick as icing on homemade cinnamon buns, like the ones Betsy served me for breakfast the last time I spent the night on Brogden Road. Everywhere I look, a memory, a flashback, a heartbreak. Sarah meets me at the airport. Ninety minutes later, we walk through the doors of Smithfield's Johnson Memorial Hospital.

I spend my hours by her side, stroking her hand, her hair. Nighttime hours and daytime. Bill Joe St. Peter is with me, or Aunt Susan or Jessie. Betsy's friend Helen comes and we pray the rosary together, slowly savoring each word, finding comfort in the familiar. "Pray for us sinners, now and at the hour of our death."

A keening rises from somewhere deep within me. Its sound slowly loosening my throat, pushing upward through each chakra, pulsing through each muscle, each vein. My blood carrying its sound, a sustained note of sorrow and loss. My mother is dying. My mama. And she called for me. Wanted me with her. No longer afraid.

The first day passes, and then the second. And on the second day, more cousins arrive. Cousins who live farther away or who were away at school, like Charli and Traci and Andi, Aunt Susan's grandchildren. I meet my Uncle Bill's daughters. And I, first born of all the Sanders grandchildren, taste for the first time the beauty and warmth of Mary and Patsy and Jenny and Helen and Theresa. I love them immediately, these women I would have grown up with, lived next door to, had things been different. All of us gather around my mother's bed. Sharing stories and quiet and prayer.

At three o'clock, Betsy stops breathing. Mary opens the window to set her spirit free.

Chapter Twenty-Three

That evening Aunt Susan and I go to Mass at Betsy's beloved St. Ann's. There is an audible gasp from the congregation as her death is announced, her life so intricately bound up with theirs. I can feel eyes on me, feel their wondering about who stood so tall next to the familiar figure of Susan Barbour. Aunt Susan introduces me as Betsy's daughter as women and men came to offer sympathy. I witness the fumbling and graceful recovery of these dear people as their perception of Betsy changes, even as her very way of existing has changed.

Uncle Bill and Aunt Susan make the decision to include my name as surviving daughter in Betsy's obituary, along with her seven grandchildren and four great-grandchildren. I'm not sure they realize all the calls that decision will generate from people who think a mistake has been made.

"Betsy didn't have no daughter," Beulah proclaims, spokesperson for the many who did not know our story.

Yet they are gracious, all the wonderful people who come to the wake to honor Betsy, welcoming both myself and my daughter Aimee, who has driven from Charlotte to be with me – to say her own goodbyes to her grandmother. "You both look so familiar," they say in one way or another. "I wish Betsy hadn't felt the need to keep you a secret."

To meet Betsy's friends, more family—it is both overwhelming and healing. I can't help thinking how Betsy would have enjoyed orchestrating it all.

After the wake we gather with all the Sanders clan at the family farmhouse. 2810 Brogden Road. Betsy's place. The home where she was born. The home she returned to in 1945. Of course we would gather there.

Here I listen as my cousins tell me of their experiences growing up. About picking cotton and how hard it was, and harvesting tobacco and learning the ins and outs of farm machinery. How when they came of a certain age, my mother would take them to Emerald Isle on the Eastern shores of North Carolina, introducing them to both camping and fishing. How she commandeered an old school bus and transformed it into a place of laughter and fun and shelter on the lot she bought five minutes from the sea. She taught them how to bait a hook and not to be squeamish about it. And how to safely catch puffer fish and handle other exotic sea creatures. It seemed to them that Betsy's knowledge knew no limits. Her passion, the sea. And she shared it generously. I love listening to them, absorbing their love for my mother. Hoping they will love me as well.

Chapter Twenty-Four

Aunt Susan invites me to choose the readings and the music for Betsy's funeral. Betsy had once told me about a young friend of hers, Kathy Pittman, who played the guitar and whose music she loved, and I invite her to play for Betsy. Annie, one of Betsy's great-nieces, is asked to read from the "Introduction to the Reissued Nancy Drew Series" – that wonderful tribute written by Margaret Maron. Bill Joe is chosen to give the eulogy. And because I know it was important to my mother, it gives me great comfort to find out that there will be three priests upon the altar of St. Ann's to celebrate her Mass of Resurrection. It is a beautiful ceremony, full of meaning and solace.

Our last ritual for Betsy takes place three days later. On that day her ashes are taken to Smithfield's only cemetery. Just a few of us are able to be there. Bill Joe, Jessie, Aunt Susan, Uncle Bill, and myself.

We watch as the funeral director digs a small hole in ground that seems unreasonably hard. He is an elderly man and the effort leaves him breathless, yet he will accept no help. The parish priest offers prayers, then steps back as if conscious that his role is complete.

Before we left the house on Brogden Road that morning, Aunt Susan shared with me my mother's last request.

"She wanted showers of sea shells placed on her grave," she said and led me to the back porch where jars of shells overflowed shelves lined with oil cloth. "Choose some."

And now I step forward, the first to shower shells upon my mother's grave.

Chapter Twenty-Five

On my last evening in Smithfield, we sit around a small table on Jessie's back porch. Just Jessie and Bill Joe and myself—the self-proclaimed night owls. How at home I feel. Drinking wine, offering toasts to Betsy, talking about the people who came to the wake, the Mass—Jessie and Bill Joe helping me keep names and relationships straight.

"Does Dianne know all her mothers?" Bill Joe asks with a glance at Jessie.

"I don't think she does," she says.

Without further discussion, Bill Joe takes pen in hand and starts writing:

Elizabeth Bynum Sanders, 1913 – 2000
Mary Bynum Peterson, 1889 – 1966
Agnes Alwyn Watson, 1855 – 1911
Mary Ann Higdon, 1814 – 1864
Elizabeth Rogers, 1797 – 1844
Charlotta Bowlin-Temple

He hands the paper to me. "These are all your mothers."

My fingers tingle as I accept the lined paper from Bill Joe's hand, my breath quickening as I read the names over and over, pronouncing each one distinctly as if they were royalty. Here, in black and white, my line of ancestry. My own "begats". And I know then, with a deep and authentic knowing that yes, I am legitimate.

I have come home.

Epilogue

March 18, 2012 is the twelfth anniversary of Betsy's death.

My husband Frank and I are vacationing in Panama, staying in a small town called Playa Corona. I am sitting on the balcony of our rented studio, overlooking the Pacific Ocean. Orange and pink bands scatter across the sky, casting soft light on the lush bougainvillea that frame the deck. Sunrise, and I can already feel the heat of day.

I watch mesmerized as waves form close to shore, unfurl one after the other, and gently tap the sand like an affectionate lover. It is low tide, and fingers of rocks and pebbles are exposed, extending beyond my sight around the bluffs to my right. Five white egrets step placidly amid the crevices, a sharp contrast to the blackened volcanic sand and stone.

But it is the tidal pools that draw me—shallow pools, crammed with cowries and chitins clinging to uneven ridges. Here oyster shells clasp stones—a marriage of forces. Soon sun-browned young men will gather the shell fish for market, but for now I am alone.

Sea sounds weave into my very bones, thrum through my pores, give rhythm to my step. I have a sense of being lighter than air, wrapped in the color of sunrise, my eyes focused in wonder. And I know this is Betsy's legacy.

Today I see her reflection in each tidal pool. Hear her voice instructing *me* on all the teeming life within.

And I am grateful.

Acknowledgements

With love and appreciation for the late Helen and Bill Flore, adoptive parents extraordinaire, who gifted me with family, education and so much love. And for my brothers Bill and Gene and my sister Kathleen, all younger.

A profound thank you to my husband Frank for his unending love and support and to each of our seven children: Danielle, Erika, Aimee, Fran, Tim, Chris and Matt. In so many ways my journey has been your journey as well.

With appreciation for the Sisters of St. Joseph of Buffalo, who staffed "Our Lady of Victory Home" in Lackawanna, New York. Special thanks to Sisters Margaret Manzella, Madelene Stauring, Cecile Ferland and the late Jane Boudreau who were ever available with their listening hearts and a cup of coffee as I stepped into the waters of finding Miss Betsy. In her roles as spiritual director and friend, Sr. Joan Wagner brought both perspective and healing to help keep me afloat.

I am grateful to the late Mary Del Tramont, whose search for her own birth mother led me to PACES, Post Adoption Center for Education and Support, and the sincere encouragement of others on the same journey to wholeness. In particular, I salute Kathryn Blake, Mary Fay, Ray Ranic, Ann and the late Kenneth Schmitt and Joan Weaver, author of "Forbidden Family".

I offer heartfelt thanks to Margaret Maron for her words about my mother published as the introduction of Applewood Books' reissued Nancy Drew mystery, "The Clue in the Diary" and especially, her permission to reprint them. Through her tribute to Miss Betsy, I not only understood my mother better, but also gained an intimate glimpse of life in the rural South which formed my family as well.

Thanks to Marjorie Norris who inspired me with her poem "When She Got Born" from her collection entitled "Two Suns, Two Moons" published by Aventine Press.

Julie Cameron, author of "The Artist's Way", refers to people in her writing circles as "believing mirrors". I have been graced with many "believing mirrors". First among them is Patricia McClain who invited me to the Canisius College Writing Workshops facilitated by Barbara Faust and Tom O'Malley. Here, in the company of so many talented writers, including Mary Ellen Feron (Zablocki), author of the "A Tent for the Sun. A Story of Extraordinary Love", I began to take my writing seriously.

But it is both the "Women of the Vineyard" and the "Writers of Café 59," intrepid and gifted women of depth and wisdom, who exemplify the role of "believing mirrors." I am so fortunate to have each of you in my life: Evelyn Brady, Ginger Cunningham, Mary Callahan, Elly Cannito, Mary Herbst, Patricia McClain, Fredda McDonald, Marjorie Norris, Carol Pasiecznik, Sarah Ries, Kathy Shoemaker and Ann Walsh.

Over the years my Book Club has served as sounding boards, continually encouraging my quest to bring the story of Betsy to print. Along with Mary Herbst and Patty McClain, Mary Durward, Mary Joan Eberhardt, Kathleen Heffern, Patricia LaFalce, Judy McDermid, Linda Murphy and Catherine Zalocha have enriched my life in ways too numerous to count. Each of you individually and all of you together are a treasure trove of "believing mirrors."

I offer bouquets of gratitude to my unofficial editors who generously and graciously spent countless hours going over each line, bringing the story to a new level of completion. You are my heros: Evelyn Brady, Mary Joan Eberhardt, Rosalind Giallela, Mary Herbst and Patty McClain. I am grateful, too, for the unbridled and loving enthusiasm of Jasmin Pixley as I shared with her my chapters or my poetry.

Thanks to Pip Wallace, my account manager, who walked me through all things technical with great patience, and to my editor and design team at FriesenPress for the attention and care given my words.

Finally, I raise a toast to my mother Betsy, whose courage and openness made everything possible. I am glad for both of us.

Printed in Canada